Follow the Yellow Brick Road

(One minute)

Page 81   10/21/12
You called me
Still adore   9/20
P   .   9/13
     131 + 137
God let you slumber
continue
You control the climate

Page
211
Fair boat
Its my desire   desire
              8/11
         8/13/13
         P.170

I gave me

174
Prague
Moving out
The blood of
Jesus

FOLLOW the YELLOW BRICK ROAD

Reba Rambo-McGuire
with
Judy A. Gossett

Page 96.
For Misty
Don't give up —

Page 215
Favorite
Psalm 37
Love in
KJV

6/10/13
98 —

Page
46 — 99 —
For Jimi
Faqueros.
Jamis

Page 140 —

Page 202
Favorite
A perfect heart

Page
13
2nd half.
9/22

Starting
Page 53
on Baal
Baal / Good & Involuntary

Page 134
For Jamus
Favorite
6/11/13

Great
Poem
Page 80
agree to disagree
Misti

Page 90
Ounce of Prevention is
worth a pound of cure

Follow the Yellow Brick Road

Fresh Bread

An Imprint of

Destiny Image® Publishers, Inc.

P.O. Box 310
Shippensburg, PA 17257-0310

ISBN 0-7684-5010-1
Library of Congress Catalog Card Number: 2001 132714

For Worldwide Distribution
Printed in the U.S.A.

This book and all other Destiny Image, Revival Press, MercyPlace, Fresh Bread, Destiny Image Fiction, and Treasure House books are available at Christian bookstores and distributors worldwide.

For a U.S. bookstore nearest you, call **1-800-722-6774.**
For more information on foreign distributors, call **717-532-3040.**
Or reach us on the Internet: **www.destinyimage.com**

DEDICATION

To Dony

You sprinkle my life with song,
I drink in every phrase.
You are the love of my life
and the life of my love.

God moves by atmosphere
You control the Climate by
the words you speak

#31

Linus y your Family Panot Sold
to the town gosip

Reba's Acknowledgments

No one succeeds alone. When I began compiling my "thank you" list and it was approaching novel length, I realized there was no way to acknowledge every person woven into the tapestry of my life. Please forgive me for not mentioning all of you who are silver and gold threads amongst the muslin. You know who you are.

I am eternally grateful to:

— My first love, Jesus Christ. I have come to know you as Savior, Healer, Lord, and Summit Dancer. You are The Voice who is always whispering in the whirlwind.

— My remarkable husband, Dony. I believe in miracles because of you. You hold my heart in your hands.

— My three laughing children—Dionne, Destiny, and Israel and adorable new son-in-law, Scott. Generations and nations will be transformed because of you. You are my "estachios"!

— My indescribable mother, Dottie Rambo, the greatest living lyricist of Christian music. Your courage amidst adversity is an inspiration to me and the world. (Maybe I'll be like you when I grow up.) I love you to the moon and back again.

— My wonderful father, Buck Rambo, and Mae. Thank you for your unconditional love and encouragement. Dad, I'll never outgrow the need to snuggle in your arms.

— My right arm, Cindy, for the thousand little things you do every day. You are the ultimate!

— Joel, Sandy (my little gazelle), Zach, Alex, and Andy. Thanks for guarding the stuff and reminding me of what's important.

— Dusty, LaVonne, and Miss Katie...forever faithful.

— The McGuires for loving me as daughter and sister.

— Uncle Donald, Aunt Betty and all the Rambo and Luttrell clans in Kentucky who taught me the meaning of family.

— Master craftsmen who molded the clay when it was young: Mother; Phil Johnson; Fred Carter; Andraé Crouch; Madeleine L'Engle; Bill and Gloria Gaither; and Al Kasha. If I am acknowledged as a writer at all, it is because of you.

— Life-changing mentors who have gone Home, forever embedding pieces of yourselves in my heart. You marked the trail for me: my beloved teacher, Mrs. Flossie Jepson; author, poet, and shepherd, Bob Benson; my first record producer and eternal provoker, Bob McKenzie; arranger and big brother, R.D. Karraker; my fun-loving brother-in-law, Jerry McGuire (you would be so proud of Joan and Candra).

— Sisterhood girlfriends whose friendships are touchstones in my life: Bree, Susan, Cynthia, Sandra, Lola, and Pam.

— The leadership and growing church family at *The River At Music City*. Dony and I are so blessed to pastor such excellent people who are reaching Nashville and the nations for God.

— The great staff of Rambo-McGuire Ministries, Inc.

— Denise Gerrich for endless hours of research.

— Destiny Image Publishers for taking a risk on Judy and me.

— Our buddy, Tommy Tenney, for opening the doors at Destiny Image...and for making us hungry to chase and catch God.

— Test readers who proofed several drafts of the manuscript.

— Spiritual fathers who have guarded my soul: Rev. Jimmy Russell, Rev. Roland Gardner, Bishop Earl Paulk, Dr. Ron Halvorson, and Rev. Ray McCollum.

— The five-fold ministries who unselfishly pour into my life.

— Special thanks to Drs. Rodney and Adonica Howard-Browne for fathering revival into us. We'll never be the same!

— Covenant pastors linked arm-and-arm with Dony and me. The gold bracelet each of you wears testifies of our eternal gratitude and commitment to our relationship.

— Our spiritual children, now numbering in the dozens. Thank you for enduring Dony and me as your parents. So often I have wondered, "Who are the teachers? You or us?" If you don't achieve greater things than Dony and me, we have failed. Always remember: we believe in you.

— The ministry partners whose prayerful support enables Dony and me to touch the world for Jesus.

— Dr. Tom and Maureen Anderson for the mountain getaway.

— My forever friends I know I can still call at 2 a.m.

— My chosen sister, Judy—the walking *Strong's Concordance*. If we were in quicksand to our eyeballs...

flanked by blood-thirsty anacondas and razor-teethed crocodiles...ravenous, salivating cannibals stalking the edge of the pit...you'd just wink, magically produce a *Kleenex* for me and insist, "Now what does the Word say about this, F.A.?" That's what I love about you, Jude. I wouldn't change a thing about you. Shall we click our heels and pen another adventure?

JUDY'S ACKNOWLEDGMENTS

The Lord Jesus Christ for breathing Your Life and Love into mine. It's in You I live, move, and have my being. How I love You!

My awesome father, mentor, and general-of-the-faith, Dr. Don Gossett; his wife, Debra; my siblings Michael, Jeanne, Donnie, Marisa and Sally; brothers-in-law Ken and Ken; sister-in-law Shelley; the next generation Jen, Alexander and Kristian; Vanessa, Jessica, Rebekah and Samantha; Brandon, Jordan and Justin; Victoria and James. You are my treasures. I love you.

Friends of a lifetime: my chosen brother, Dony McGuire; Destiny, Israel and Dionne; Cindy; Andraé and Sandra; Pattie and Shekinah; Angie; Daniel; the Salomons; Garth and Debbie; Alton and Sophia; Heron and Marcia; Michaela; Gerard and Charlene; Rick and Joan; Ross and Brenda; Jenn; Terri; Ray and Pam; David, Nicole, and Lisa. My spiritual mentors: T.L. Osborn; Pastors Bob and Joan Seymour; Drs. Ron and Annie Halvorson; Tommy Tenney; Dr. D.G.S. Dhinakaran; the Hinns and all the anointed ministers, singers, musicians, and authors whose God-giftings have indelibly marked my life.

Posthumously: my beloved mother, encourager, and prototype of faith, Joyce A. Gossett, who died in my arms on August 11, 1991; missionary and mentor, Dr. Daisy Osborn, who went to be with Jesus on May 27, 1995; my dear friends and Kingdom warriors, Pastors Joe and Linda Knight, who rode off into the sunset together during the Alaska Airlines #261 crash on January 31, 2000. Each of you lives on in Reba and me.

The sister-of-my-heart, Reba Rambo-McGuire. Thank you for more than 30 years of *you*. Your intimate relationship with Jesus challenges me; your hungry pursuit of His glory awes me; your prophetic eye sears me; your amazing voice thrills me; your butterfly mind fascinates me; your loving trust in Dony delights me. You are God's gift—and my forever friend. I love you, F.A.

CONTENTS

Foreword   xv
Judy's Prologue   xvii
Chapter 1   In the Beginning   1
Chapter 2   The Courtroom   17
Chapter 3   Life Before Oprah   23
Chapter 4   Skeletons in the Closet   31
Chapter 5   The Wind Began to Switch   41
Chapter 6   Tragedy Strikes   49
Chapter 7   Guilt and Shame   59
Chapter 8   Half a Woman Attracts Half a Man . .   81
Chapter 9   "Lord, Change Me"   97
Chapter 10 I Decide What I Wear   117
Chapter 11 God's Oxygen   129
Chapter 12 Bomb Your Enemy   141
Chapter 13 The Poppy Field   151
Chapter 14 The Castle Dungeon   157
Chapter 15 What's Love Got to Do With It?   167
Chapter 16 If I Only Had a Heart   179
Chapter 17 If I Only Had a Brain   203
Chapter 18 Courage of a Lion   217
Reba's Epilogue There's No Place Like Home   233
Appendix   241

FOREWORD

arely do poets publicly display their private pain. Most of the time they choose to make transparent observations of someone else or someplace else. This is the public story of a poet's private journey—a road map, if you please. With rich words and deep truths, Reba and Judy have put on public display the x-ray of a "heart."

At first you'll think, "I'm glad that wasn't me"; but by the end of this book you'll be saying, "That's just like me."

I must warn you—nothing is left out! Every bend and every bump in the road is noted. This map of lives changed includes enough detail so you will be able to avoid some "bumps" yourself. I love good writing. But true stories well written are even better. This is "good writing"—but a better story.

Tommy Tenney
Author, GodChaser

JUDY'S PROLOGUE

～ *1982* ～

How dare Dony McGuire look like Jesus!

Dony's saintly white linen shirt billowed softly in the Santa Ana breeze in stark contrast
to the dingy graffiti backdrop. His long black hair and
beard, sun-bronzed skin, and piercing eyes emitted a quiet
confidence I had never seen in him before.

But then again, he had always been a great actor.

The only reason I had agreed to drive into the no-
man's land of this dangerous southcentral L.A. housing
project was Reba had begged and bugged me.

Curious residents peered over dilapidated wrought-
iron balconies of the high-rise apartment complex into the
common grounds below. Cool teenaged boys, half-hidden
behind rusty trash dumpsters, traded hits on a glass pipe
as *Soul Train* wanna-be girls clad in tie-dyed halter-tops
and velvet hot pants flirted nearby. A handful of dirty-faced

kids straight out of *The Little Rascals* took turns riding a huge, mangy Heinz 57 dog around a rickety park bench, poking fun at the ancient wino trying to catch a nap.

An old borrowed flatbed truck-turned-makeshift-stage, anchored by gargantuan speakers projecting the booming sound for blocks, was an unusual sight in this forgotten corner of the concrete jungle. A couple of Grammy-winning artists backed by a kicking band and singers were even greater oddities. The crowd of several hundred was drawn like moths to a flame, swaying, dancing, and listening in spite of themselves.

I mingled among the people to be invisible for a while, to observe this performance without Dony and Reba knowing I was there. I didn't want him trying to impress me.

Dony took the microphone off the stand and strode to the edge of the stage like a man on a mission. "I was a junkie...a drug dealer...an alcoholic who messed around on my wife," he admitted bluntly.

Well, at least he's telling the truth now.

"A few months ago, I passed out in the slammer and woke up when another drunk started urinating in my face," Dony continued. "I looked around that hell-hole and thought, *I wasn't born for this...*"

Dony had their attention.

Mine too.

There was something raw, transparent and real in his voice. What was it? Compassion? Unconditional love? Truth?

How dare Dony McGuire sound like Jesus!

After all the pain, broken promises, dysfunction, insanity.

Nope. I wasn't buying it.

*D*uring the next few moments, a series of small miracles occurred.

Dony conveyed his story without pretense or excuses.

Stragglers moved closer.

Angels corralled noisy children.

The cloud of witnesses took notes.

Heaven held its breath.

*S*omebody moved.

It was a background singer handing a crumpled *Kleenex* to Reba, who has never in her life had a tissue when she needed one.

Reba stood off to the side of the stage watching Dony. She was part of the scene, yet somehow removed.

That otherworld quality reminded me of the first time I met her.

1968.

I was an aggressive teenager on assignment from a Vancouver, British Columbia, radio station at the National Quartet Convention held in Tennessee. Of all the artists I interviewed, Reba was the worst. Everyone else gushed with undisguised self-promotion, offering more details about their latest albums, songs, and tours than I really cared to know.

But Reba?

She just looked beyond me and issued barely audible one-word answers into my tape recorder. I thought she was an aloof prima donna. An ice princess who couldn't be touched.

Months later, my image of Reba changed when she and I ended up on the same tour with Andraé Crouch and The Disciples.

Late one night, Andraé's twin sister, Sandra, called me into the hotel room she shared with Reba. Apparently, Reba had all the symptoms of food poisoning. Raging fever. Nausea. Commode-hugging sick.

"I called you because this girl is really bad off and you know how to pray the Word," Sandra explained wearily.

As I looked at Reba lying there in agony, clutching a pillow to her stomach, so weak, so helpless, so pathetic...I realized my ice princess perception was wrong.

She was just shy and insecure.

Compassion welled inside me and I prayed what my Daddy would call "a strong prayer of faith" filled with every healing Scripture I could remember. Reba drifted off to a peaceful sleep for a few moments and woke up healed. It was great!

Andraé had heard Reba was sick and came to check on her.

While Andraé Crouch is world famous as an incredibly talented singer and songwriter, most people don't know he is also one of the craziest, funniest men alive. (He's a few fries short of a Happy Meal.) If you've got a problem, Andraé's solution is making you laugh until your problem's not so big anymore.

Reba carried a wig on tour for the times she didn't want to deal with her long, Indian hair. She named her wig Matilda. (Don't ask.) This particular night, Matilda had been hung limply over a dresser-top lamp, weirdly illuminated by a flickering 40-watt bulb. When Andraé spied Matilda, he automatically plunked it on his head. For the next two hours, he entertained us with wild, hilarious impersonations of Tina Turner, Tiny Tim, Cher, Dottie

Rambo, Cousin It, and every other longhaired performer he could think of. Sandra, Reba, and I roared hysterically until a hotel security guard tapped on the door and warned us to keep it down.

Something wonderful happens when you laugh together.

Something wonderful happens when you pray together.

A forever covenant relationship was forged that memorable night. For more than three decades, Reba and I have been the best of friends. We've gone to hell and back together. Reba says I am the sister she always wanted. (Let me put it to you this way: I was maid of honor at both of her weddings. Okay?)

· ∽ ∾ ·

1982.

I glanced at Reba standing on the side of the ghetto stage. Her eyes shone with unmistakable love, admiration and wonder over the apparent changes in her husband. For months, she had tried to convince me of the transformation in Dony, but I was too angry and stubborn to believe it.

I'd heard the wind blow before.

How could she be so gullible? How could she possibly forget all of his lies, mind games, and abuses? How many pieces of her shattered heart would I have to help pick up this time?

But something in Dony's voice was breaking through my stony heart. Something in his tears resonated with a holy conviction that can only be birthed from a face-to-face encounter with God.

"...Jesus walked into the room and said, *'I'm not mad at you. I only want to love you'...*" Dony wept unashamedly. "I didn't deserve it, but He saved me because of love. Let me tell you something. If God could deliver a messed-up sinner like me, I know there's nothing He can't do for you!"

Dony made the love of Jesus sound so simple even a child could understand. Something beyond mere words was reaching and touching the people around me. Tears of compassion flowed freely down his face as he compelled them to come to Jesus.

How dare Dony McGuire weep like Jesus!

Teenaged girls with mascara running down their cheeks hurried forward. A whole family knelt on the dusty blacktop. Some of the boys stepped from behind dumpsters and pushed through the crowd, surrendering their drug paraphernalia on the edge of the stage. Grandmas in floral housecoats, faded slippers, and pink sponge rollers left their vinyl lawn chairs and became spontaneous altar workers.

The last traces of my icy resistance melted as I watched Agape-filled, Spirit-led Dony McGuire take a sobbing teenaged boy in his arms and lead him to Jesus.

A darling Spanky look-alike tugged at my sleeve.

"Lady, is that Jesus up on that stage?"

Looking down at his dirty, tear-streaked face into those big, hopeful eyes, I realized I was crying too.

"No, little buddy," I croaked. "That's Dony McGuire. He's a man of God."

·‿ ‿·

2001.

I never thought those words would ever come out of my mouth. "Dony McGuire" and "man of God" just didn't fit together. But when Dony was radically saved and delivered by God's power, I got knocked off my high horse. The life-change in Dony is real and undeniable. I love and trust him completely. And that's amazing to me.

During these last two decades, I have eye witnessed the incredible transformation in both Dony and Reba. They have made a quantum leap from their horrific past. The people they were...died (see Gal. 2:20[1]).

They are dead men walking.

Dony and Reba have taken great risks in stripping off the customary niceties and religious garb to stand transparent and vulnerable. *Follow the Yellow Brick Road* is their story. It is awesome proof of God's love and forgiveness, His redemption and restoration. Is their marriage perfect? No. But they are in hot pursuit of the One who is perfect.

"We fall down...we get up."[2]

How do you distill two lives into a few pages? You start at the beginning with a few basic rules. As Reba and I first outlined this book, we established three criteria.

First of all, the final manuscript had to be something Dony and Reba's three children could live with.

Secondly, the story had to help people, otherwise there would be no point in dredging up and reliving their painful past.

Thirdly, we had to truthfully transition Dony from the sick drug addict/alcoholic he used to be...to the man of God with high integrity and character he is today. If our readers were turned off—or became unable to receive from Dony because of this book—we would have failed miserably and done him a terrible injustice. Actually, he is the one who insisted this book be written. (Now that's a secure man.)

King David probably wasn't thrilled to have his acts of adultery and murder canonized in the Bible, but look at the inspiration, help, and hope countless millions have received from reading those vivid passages of Scripture. The inside of his heart was laid bare...forever. David is proof that God's hand can rest upon your life even when you're not living right. Why? Because God sees the end from the beginning. He sees His completed work.

If David could rise above his past—so can we.

Several years ago, Dony and Reba put their necks on the line by sharing their not-so-pretty saga in couples' retreats and men or women's meetings. They were blown away by the unexpected, unprecedented impact on people's lives.

Yes, we all love a good story with a happy ending, but this book's real treasure is in the simple truths and answers...the "Golden Stepping Stones"...God revealed.

This book's unconventional format—blending personal story with meaty teaching—is deliberate. In selected chapters, we have included teachings—the "Golden Stepping Stones" of the Yellow Brick Road—while omitting them from other chapters to accelerate the flow of the story. To borrow Reba's hillbilly-eze, *"The testimony's the gravy and the teachin's the prime rib."* The teachings are hot off the grill! As Reba and I researched and wrote, Holy Spirit sovereignly opened our eyes to fresh new revelations. We were catapulted into a supernatural flow beyond our natural abilities.

Because of the intense, cataclysmic subject matter, *Follow the Yellow Brick Road* isn't appropriate reading for young children. PG—parental discretion is advised. The language, authentic and graphic at points, was not written to be deliberately offensive. Actually, much of it has been toned down from the original R-rating. Certain names have been changed to protect the identity of the inno-cent...and the guilty. We have handpicked Reba's original poetry and song lyrics to enhance your chapter-to-chapter journey.

Writing *Follow the Yellow Brick Road* with Reba has been a great personal joy, a labor of love and a wild ride. We have run the gamut: Pacing the floor at 4:00 in the morning dressed in flannel pajamas in our agonizing search for the *perfect word*. Chewing thousands of pieces of Super Bubble. Single-handedly rescuing the forest industry by using mountains of paper to print our manuscript drafts. Boosting the stock market value of Canon BC1-11 printer cartridges. Pushing our friendship to new limits.

We have been deeply moved: Mascara to our toenails. Worshipful awe. Gut-rot. Hyena laughing until we were hoarse. (At least, page 121, "not in the mood ..." was funny to us.)

We have written and edited over the phone. On scraps of napkins at restaurants. In the backseat of a speeding taxi in India. On Dony and Reba's tour bus. Thirty-nine thousand feet high on a flight from New Zealand. In tiny hotel bathrooms so as not to disturb Dony sleeping in the next room. Worn out two laptop computers...(Not that Reba ever learned to use one.)

We have fought the fear of rejection and censure from religious critics. We have seriously questioned, "Is this any good or are we just crazy?" More than once, Dony had to rescue the manuscript—and us—from a trashcan. If you look closely, you will see blood, tears, and Starbucks coffee staining each page.

·ᵕ ᵕ·

*R*eferences and allusions to Reba's childhood favorite, *The Wizard of Oz*, are interwoven throughout the tapestry of this book.

L. Frank Baum was interviewed after writing *The Wizard of Oz* series. He was asked, "Where did the name Oz come from?"

"I was sitting behind my desk trying to come up with the perfect title when I glanced up at a file cabinet," he grinned sheepishly. "The top drawer was labeled "A-N" and the bottom one "O-Z"...*The Wizard of An* didn't seem to work, but *Oz* rang a bell."

In writing *Follow the Yellow Brick Road*, Reba has rung a few bells of her own. She has dared open a few top-secret files from her private life. Because she is a born storyteller, this book is the first in her own series of adventures.

Grab a handful of tissues and join Reba for what promises to be a momentous journey. You'll soon discover—like Dorothy—Reba Rambo-McGuire is permanently "off to see the wizard." But as her award-winning song acknowledges, *He's so much more than a wizard...and He can make new creatures out of us.*[3]

Endnotes

1. "Having considered that I've died, I now enjoy a second existence which is simply Jesus using my body" (Gal. 2:20 The Abbreviated Translation, 1901. Taken from version used by Bible Explorer on Epiphany Software).

2. "We Fall Down" by Matthew Kyle David. BMG Songs Inc. / ASCAP. Used by permission.

3. "The Land of Ooh's and Ah's" by Reba Rambo. Copyright 1977. Heartwarming Music / BMI. Used by permission.

"The Lady Is a Child"

The moment I first learned to talk
I tried to say Your name
Then I drew Your face with squeaky chalk
on a slate in my nursery games
I loved to sing the little songs 'bout
"Climb, Climb the Sunshine Mountain"
and paste Your pictures in a book
where You blessed the little children

Then I grew up
and now I speak with lines rehearsed
They choose to call me "Lady"
and a lady's lovely
(so I've heard)
They pinned gardenias in my hair
dressed me in gowns of satin
But do they see the little girl
hiding there behind the silk fan?

'Cause when I'm with You
The Lady's still a little child
I love to snuggle up in Your arms
and just listen to You talk
It don't matter much
if I'm all dressed up
or in my old blue jeans
As long as in my heart
The Lady is a child[a]

Chapter 1

IN THE BEGINNING

~ *Reba* ~

We were so poor — poor people called us poor.

My family was born and raised in the coal mining regions of southwestern Kentucky. We often lived with Daddy's parents, Ma and Pa Rambo, in Walnut Grove, population 36. Hee-haw! Dawson Springs, population 3800, was only a few miles down the road, but to get there, you had to "go to town."

Instead of four bedrooms and three baths, we had four rooms and a path...to the three-hole, quarter-moon outhouse about fifty yards from the back porch. Mosquito-bitten legs dangling over the splintery, roughhewn ledge, my young girl cousins—Peggy, Kathy, Barbara and Sandy—and I would "do our business" and pore through the ever-dwindling *Sears and Roebuck* catalogue to distract us from the foul, fly-infested mound steaming below. We memorized our favorite pages, salivating over romantic fashions, new-fangled gadgets, top-of-the-line appliances and most importantly, indoor plumbing. Ma always ripped out the "brassieres and girdles" section to help keep curious young boys from sinning.

There were 13 children in Daddy's family, 11 in Mother's...and I was an only child.

Go figure.

At the ripe old age of 18 months, I made my radio debut singing "When the Saints Go Marchin' In." Now you know that was a performance even Pavarotti would envy!

As a small child, I recognized the growing call of God for music ministry in my parents. Mother's raven-haired beauty, innate songwriting talent, and contagious effervescence created a born communicator. Daddy's country boyish charm, velvet smooth voice, and astute business acumen propelled them into ever-increasing popularity.

When I was three years old, my parents quit their day jobs and packed our few but freshly starched clothes in *Pet Milk* cardboard boxes and stashed them into a worn-out 1948 Plymouth station wagon. With one revival booked, a couple of second-hand guitars and a pocketful of dreams, we took off to win the world for Jesus.

Night after night, Daddy lifted my ruffled, crinolined frame onto rickety piano benches of churches throughout our area and I sang "In My Father's House Are Many Mansions" or another song Mother wrote just for me, entitled "There's Only One Door to Heaven."

For an already sheltered, insecure little girl, I was overwhelmed by people's unrealistic expectations of me being "the perfect evangelists' child." The pressure took its toll and gradually forced me deeper into my imaginary world. Besides, riding for hundreds of miles on slick tires and sleeping in musty church basements wasn't really my idea of a good time.

I was torn between the yearning to be with Mother and Daddy wherever they were...the demands of people on the road...my love for the beautiful, rolling hills and simple lifestyle at home...and the dark secrets buried in our close-knit little community.

The dilemma was resolved when I started first grade and we opted for the normalcy of public school.

While there was always an abundance of family willing to take me—in reality, I never quite fit in.

I was a loner.

My greatest sense of belonging was found in the sanctuary of the lush forests just beyond my grandparents' acreage.

Before daybreak, I crammed my red-and-white checkerboard knapsack with cathead biscuits lathered with sorghum molasses, my trusty pocketknife, a dog-eared Big Chief notepad and a fat yellow pencil I sharpened by whittling the point. Tiptoeing out of the slumbering house, I tossed some scraps and soup bones into the wire pen to keep Pa's prize 'coon dogs from barking. Grabbing a handful of matches and a coal-oil lantern off the porch, I plodded through the damp fields.

My mission was to penetrate the heart of the forest before the morning sun peaked over the sloping hills.

I hurried to the best seat in the house: a massive, moss-covered stump conveniently perched beside a gushing artesian spring. I claimed my gnarly throne from which I sampled the inevitable Epicurean feast.

Since Adam ruled Eden, no experience has equaled the pure exhilaration of the fresh awakening of dew-kissed woods.

Follow the Yellow Brick Road

The symphony of morning sounds...
  Whispering zephyrs
    Parachuting whirlybirds
      Snapping twigs
        Warbling robins
  Buzzing insects
    Scampering critters
      Gurgling rivulets
        Swooping hawks
The ambrosia of morning savories...
  Puckering persimmons
    Staining blackberries
      Popping chanterelles
        Slurping honeysuckles
  Conniving catfish
    Crunching acorns
      Plopping crabapples
        Dripping nectars

The bouquet of morning scents...
  Ripening earth
    Invigorating peppermint
      Decaying carcasses
        Burgeoning blossoms
  Flaunting strawberries
    Overpowering onions
      Decomposing bark-mulch
        Flourishing herbs

The circumference of morning senses...
  Squishing mud-puddles
    Cushioning carpet
      Slithering earthworms
        Twisting grapevines

4

In the Beginning

Molting plumage
   Aggravating thistles
     Metamorphosing cocoons
      Trickling waters

The pageantry of morning sights...
  Vanishing shadows
    Evaporating mists
     Waving grasslands
      Evolving hues
 Oozing saps
   Dilating buds
     Colonizing fire-ants
      Fluttering butterflies[1]

I danced with creation, a splendid smile curling the corners of my mouth as I envisioned Ma Rambo applauding my uniqueness.

She said I was her butterfly child.

⁎⁎⁎

J'm not exactly sure when Germs showed up, but it seems like he was always there. This dingy-gray, pint-sized, shaggy-haired dog was my very best friend.

Oh, yeah. Germs was invisible too.

Although we were dirt-poor, we had very little dirt in our house. Mother was one of those "nasty nice" people who Pine-Soled everything. Armed with rubber gloves, mops, brooms, dustpans, buckets, brushes, and an industrial-strength vacuum cleaner, she launched an attack rivaling the Allied Forces invasion of Normandy on every available surface. Germs were her greatest enemy. From floor to ceiling, wall to wall, nothing escaped her sanitation frenzy. If she stayed any place more than a day, it ended up smelling like a pristinely sterilized hospital.

I so wanted to please my mother. If she came home unexpectedly and the house looked like Hurricane Camille had swept through it, I would gaze up at her with wide, innocent eyes and swear convincingly, *"I didn't do it. Germs did it!"*

Poor Germs got blamed for everything. If I came home from school with the hem falling out of my skirt, pigtails untwisted, best hair ribbon missing and my only pair of shoes all scuffed up...

"It wasn't me! Honest, Mother! Germs ran aaand... knocked me down aaand...took off with my ribbon!"

Mother would give me that raised eyebrow "Liar, Liar, pants on fire" look and assure me that—in one hour—she would set my pants on fire. She never wanted to whip me when she was angry, so she gave herself 60 minutes to cool down...and 60 minutes for me to live in hell!

I would clean the house, bake her a pie, run her a bubble bath and kneel down beside my little table and chairs and plead, "Dear God! If You've ever helped—please help me right now!"

But He didn't...and she did.

After the peach-tree switchin'—I'd go crawl up in the trundle bed and let my naughty dog have it. But how do you stay mad at a stupid dog that keeps licking your face and promising he'll do better next time?

My imaginary world was so real to me that it always amazed me when nobody else could see Germs...or the three little old ladies who came to tea each afternoon wearing elaborate hats, lace gloves, and long flowing dresses.[2]

Miss Lucy had scandalous flaming red hair with white roots showing. She flaunted Lucille Ball lipstick, smudged dots of rouge on her cheeks and chunky ear bobs, much to my delight and much to the chagrin of prim-and-proper Miss Persnickety who absolutely *never* wore make-up, but dressed in high-necked, long-sleeved black mourning clothes and always ranted and raved about the virtues of holiness. The third little lady was sweet, plump Miss Sally, a perpetual peacemaker who tried to distract the other two from their silly quarrels by cooing, *"Aren't these lovely cakes we're having today?"*

Sometimes Mother indulged me by joining Germs, the ladies and me for tea.

One rainy afternoon, Mother had fallen asleep on the couch. I shushed Germs and the ladies to keep them as quiet as possible during our afternoon ritual so Mother could nap. Suddenly the old-fashioned wall phone jangled her awake. It was our pastor's wife on the line, announcing she and a couple of the deacons' wives would be dropping by in about 15 minutes.

Instantly, Mother kicked into whirlwind cleaning mode. She barked orders to me and I barked orders to the ladies, "Clean up this mess!" Germs just barked and jumped on the couch to get out of the way.

Mother charged into the living room with her smoke-belching, fire-breathing vacuum cleaner and headed straight for the couch. I turned around just in time to see poor, terrified Germs vanish into the gaping mouth of the monstrous cleaning machine.

"Mother!! You just sucked Germs into the vacuum cleaner!!" I howled in horror.

"Reba, stop being so silly! I don't have time for this."

"But he can't breathe! He'll die in there!"

"Reba Faye, you listen to me. Germs is *not* real. He's just your imagination!"

"Yes, he *is* real...and you're killin' him! You gotta open that thing up and let him out!"

Exasperated, Mother shut off the vacuum, opened up the metal canister and released a dirty but grateful Germs into my waiting arms. The ladies applauded graciously as my frazzled mother ran to answer the pounding on the door.

$\smile$

My greatest discovery in the first grade was the school library. I had learned to read before starting elementary school and had already worn out a few hand-me-down primers.

I'll always remember cautiously turning the dull brass knob, timidly pushing open the creaking, heavy oak door and solemnly entering a galaxy of wonder.

Whoo-oo! I never knew so many books existed!

Floor to ceiling, row after row, shelf upon shelf of new friends dressed in leather and paper jackets. Boy, was I impressed!

Germs peeked his head out of my navy blue cardigan pocket to sneak a better view. I quickly stuffed him back into hiding...'cause everybody knew you weren't supposed to bring a dog to school.

I reverently crept down the first aisle, drinking in the titles and softly mouthing the impressive authors' names. Mentally calculating the contents of my piggy bank, I wondered how many extra chores I'd have to do to save up enough money to buy even one of these remarkable-sounding adventures.

A nice lady with little wire-rimmed eyeglasses asked, "May I help you?" It was Miss Laselda Hamby, the school librarian.

"Uh, how much does it cost to get one?"

"There's no charge if you return them on time," she chuckled, politely patting my head. "Two cents a day for overdues."

"How many can you take at one time?"

"Six, but that's quite a load for a little tyke like you."

Miss Laselda Hamby obviously didn't understand. I had just landed in Heaven and wouldn't be denied!

She steered me to the children's book section and I lost all track of time leafing through *The Five Little Peppers and How They Grew* and *Stuart Little*. I was sitting at a small table weeping for *The Box Car Children* when the kind librarian handed me her monogrammed handkerchief, whispering, "I know just the book for you, young lady. If you like it, there are several others in the original series by Mr. L. Frank Baum."

She stamped the library card and slipped a burgundy, leather-bound volume with gold embossed lettering...*The Wizard of Oz*...onto my growing pile of treasures. The final bell rang as I thanked her and dashed out the door.

Uncle Donald, dressed in his crisp white uniform, was waiting impatiently to pick me up in his Bunny Bread work truck, whimsically painted with a gigantic-eared rabbit that grinned foolishly, "That's what I said...Bunny Bread!" Uncle Donald lifted me and my bounty into the truck, sneaked me a little peach pie to snack on as he told corny jokes all the way to Ma's house.

What I really wanted to devour was any one of those books!

I ran up the lane, yelled a quick greeting to Ma who was working in her vegetable garden and made a beeline to my favorite indoor hideout: *the quilt closet*. I pulled back the faded, flowered drape and climbed the side shelves, carefully avoiding Mason jars filled with canned green beans, pickled beets, and blackberry jam. With *The Wizard of Oz* clutched to my chest, Germs and I gingerly sank onto the high stack of handmade patchwork quilts. I reached up and tugged on a frayed cord as the dusty, phosphorescent bulb lit up "black and white Kansas."

Germs didn't like books all that much, but when he saw the sketches of Dorothy and her constant companion, Toto, he was hooked. (Can you believe it? My silly dog had never learned to read for himself even though I tried to teach him.) But this time I didn't mind the slower pace of reading out loud to him because I wanted to savor every delicious-sounding word and phrase.

Kansas...Kentucky. They kinda sounded alike.

Aunty Em and Uncle Henry...Ma and Pa Rambo.

Toto...Germs.

Dorothy...me.

As the story unfolded, I felt as though Mr. L. Frank Baum was writing about me. But how could he know? I flipped to the inside page to see when the book was published. Circa 1900. Nope. Wasn't me. But it sure felt like it.

⁓

*J*can never forget the first time I saw the classic MGM film version of *The Wizard of Oz*, starring Judy Garland.

It was Sunday night. I was nine years old, quarantined at home with German measles and Strep throat. I had heard other kids talk about this wonderful movie, but since it usually came on Sunday night TV, I figured I'd be at least 73 by the time I saw it.

In our house on Sunday afternoons, no one ever asked, "Are we going to church tonight?" It wasn't an option. Church on Sunday morning 'n night and midweek was as natural as breathing. You had to be practically "hospital sick" to miss a meeting.

Daddy stayed home to take care of me and persuaded Mother to go ahead and lead the singing at our little country church. Hoping to distract me from the aches and pains, he gently carried me into the living room and propped me up on a mountain of goose down pillows on the sofa. A comforting, crackling fire burned in the coal grate to ward off the chill from my high fever as the unforgettable overture lifted me on butterfly wings into another time and place...somewhere over the rainbow.

⁓ ⁓

I am not a nine-year-old anymore and Germs now lives in the blue jeans pocket of my young son, Israel. I am not Mr. L. Frank Baum, but I do have a story to tell.

This is not a simple autobiography. I am probably too young for that and too many people are still alive. But I have traveled many winding roads and meandered down quite a few bunny trails. My Father has lovingly taught me indispensable life lessons and secrets—the "Golden Stepping Stones," if you will—no matter if I've kept on the path and stayed tight in the ruby slippers...or wandered into haunted forests and witches' castles. The life lessons—the "Golden Stepping Stones" of the Yellow Brick Road—are

11

the most important part of my journey to the Pearly White City.

My friend Dr. Myles Munroe often says, "God starts at the end and works backwards."

Isn't it funny how—even as a first-grader reading in the top of the quilt closet—I caught a glimpse of the spiritual parallels between *The Wizard of Oz* and my own life?

As a young contemporary Christian artist, my signature song was entitled "The Land of Ooh's & Ah's"...a tribute to the fact that—if you will only look with Spirit-eyes—you can see God in every creative work He inspires in mankind.

"The Land of Ooh's and Ah's"

Once upon a time I was caught up in a whirlwind
Spinning fast 'til at last I hit the ground
Then I met some folks with faith like little children
With words of Truth, they introduced me to their King
I put His ruby slippers on my feet, started
walking the yellow brick road
Now I'm headin' for my Home
Instead of bricks, I'll walk on streets of gold

We're off to the Pearly White City
Where all of our dreams come true
Words can't describe its splendor
It's the Land of Ooh's and Ah's
Somewhere over the rainbow
We'll see the King Jesus
He's so much more than a wizard
And He can make new creatures out of us

He can take a heart so cold as a Tin Man's
And warm it up—warm it up with His love

He can give you the courage of a Lion
To stand up—stand up in the devil's face
If you've got a mixed up Scarecrow's mind
Your thoughts He will renew
If you think there's no place like home
You should see the one He's built for you

We're off to the Pearly White City
Where all of our dreams come true
Words can't describe its splendor
It's the Land of Ooh's and Ah's
Somewhere over the rainbow
We'll see the King Jesus
He's so much more than a wizard
And He can make new creatures out of us[5]

You're probably not reading this book in a quilt closet, but as you journey through the pages there may be an experience or two where you wonder, *Is she writing about me? It sure feels like it.*

Wherever you are on your pilgrimage from Kansas to Oz and back, you may have already befriended a Scarecrow, Tin Man or Lion.

You may have been caught up in a whirlwind or two.

You may feel as though life has come crashing down.

You may not know where on earth you are, but Heaven woos, summoning you to a higher realm of destiny.

Perhaps you question like Dorothy, "How do I start for the Emerald City?"

"It's always best to start at the beginning," the enchanting Glenda smiled. "All you do is follow the Yellow Brick Road."

Endnotes

1. "Morning Symphony" by Reba Rambo-McGuire and Judy A. Gossett. 2001 Rambo-McGuire Publishing. Used by permission.

2. Years later when I read Madeleine L'Engle's classic children's novel, *A Wrinkle in Time*, I wept when the characters Mrs. Whatsit, Mrs. Who and Mrs. Which were introduced. Somebody else had seen them too! Only those crazy ladies had changed their names to protect their identities. *A Wrinkle in Time* by Madeleine L'Engle. Yearling Books, 1973.

3 "Land of Ooh's & Ah's" by Reba Rambo. Recorded on the Dove Award winning recording *Lady* on Benson Records. 1976 Heartwarming Music. Used by permission.

*"I know the thoughts and plans
that I have for you,
says the Lord,
thoughts and plans for welfare and peace
and not for evil,
to give you hope in your final outcome.
Then you will call upon Me,
and you will come and pray to Me,
and I will hear and heed you.
Then you will seek Me,
inquire for, and require Me
[as a vital necessity]
and find Me
when you search for Me
with all your heart...
I will be found by you,
says the Lord,
and I will release you from captivity
and gather you from all the nations
and all the places to which I have driven you,
says the Lord,
and I will bring you back ..."*[b]

Chapter 2

The Courtroom

⁓ 1979 ⁓

What is it about courtrooms?

My attorney was little more than a stranger in a three-piece suit ushering me into the stifling, musty courthouse overcrowded with hookers, junkies, and sad women. I was just another docket number to the tired magistrate sitting on the bench. My whole life was hanging in the balance and all he wanted was to go to lunch.

The less-than-ten-minute case seemed like an eternity of suffering in that torture chamber. The callous old judge barked out, "Divorce granted." When the gavel dropped, I jumped as terror and relief shot through my heart, followed by a slow-motion numbness.

"Divorce granted"—I pondered the irony. What a strange choice of words...as though he was bestowing an honor or handing out a gift.

The attorney secured my signature on a few documents, mechanically shook my hand and rushed off to his next victim. I had to get out of there! I couldn't breathe one more second in that suffocatingly hot, death-filled tomb. Willing my legs to carry me to the car, I fumbled with my keys, cursing under my breath.

I haggled with Insanity, "If you'll just get me out of this city, I'll let you lose it once we get to the country."

The bargain must have worked because the next thing I knew, I was in a secluded park beside the same babbling brook I used to tell secrets to as a young teenager.

The familiar, little stream was still there, but where was I? How did I lose that innocent, carefree part of me? Who was this way-over-the-edge woman and how did she get inside my body?

✦ ✦ ✦

*W*ith the car windows rolled up tightly and the radio blaring loudly, I screamed, wailed, and beat the steering wheel. I grew even more exasperated because I had to wipe my runny nose on the sleeve of my best silk suit.

"You're so stupid, Reba! You go to the funeral service of your marriage and don't even remember to bring a box of *Kleenex*," I bawled.

Spent and exhausted, I was enveloped by an eerie calm as I remembered the handgun hidden under the passenger seat. I had never liked touching it, but now the cold metal felt like a warm friend in my shaky hands.

"You could be out of your misery in less than a second," Insanity beckoned. "Come on! You are such a disappointment to everybody. Why don't you do the world a favor and end it all right here, right now?"

I ran a trembling finger over the smooth barrel, clicked open the chamber and let the shiny brass bullets fall into my palm. It would be so easy. Just one squeeze of the trigger...click...and instantly escape from the hellacious nightmare. I searched through the glove box for a pen and paper to write a note to whoever found me.

"Damn!¹ I can't even plan my own suicide!" I fumed when all I could come up with was a stub of discarded lipstick pencil and a few crumpled gasoline receipts.

"What about hell?" another Voice whispered.

"I'm living in hell!" I yelled back, tossing the useless pencil and papers to the floor.

"What about God?" the Voice persisted.

"That's what I want to know. What about God? Where is He?"

"Right here."

A drop of reality trickled into my broken heart. I turned down the volume on the radio to better hear the still, small Voice.

It had been so long.

"Even You can't fix the mess I've made," I sighed bleakly. "My life is ruined forever."

My soul was heavy with shame and hopelessness.

"I can probably never sing again. Lord, You know how people feel about a 'divorced Christian singer.' Every single concert was cancelled when they heard the news of my separation. They'll crucify me upside down now that the divorce is final," I moaned. "All that's left for me is singing country music and Mother would kill me if I did that!"

I slumped back in the seat and leaned into the rigid headrest. Peering through a blur of tears at the faithful, old brook, I questioned, "Will the pain ever go away? Will it get any better?"

Out of nowhere, the radio gradually grew louder. I sat upright, aware I hadn't touched the dial.

"Hey, what's going on? Who turned up the volume?" I asked in bewilderment.

The pure, innocent voice of a young girl quavered optimistically.

> *"The sun will come out tomorrow*
> *Bet your bottom dollar that tomorrow*
> *There'll be sun*
> *Just thinking about tomorrow*
> *Clears away the cobwebs and the sorrow*
> *'Til there's none ..."*[2]

"Tomorrow? Lord, are You trying to tell me that tomorrow my life will be better?" I languished.

At some point as a child attending Vacation Bible School, I had memorized a Scripture. What was it exactly? It went something like *"He has given you a future and a hope..."*[3]

The song continued.

> *"When I'm stuck with a day*
> *That's gray and lonely*
> *I just stick out my chin*
> *And grin and say*
> *Tomorrow, tomorrow*
> *I love you—tomorrow*
> *You're only a day away"*[4]

Peace like the warmth and comfort of my grandmother's patchwork quilt on a cold wintry morning wrapped around my aching heart.

"Tomorrow..." I exhaled. It may not mean much to some folks...but for me, it was a life preserver being tossed to a drowning woman. A scarlet thread of hope.

I placed the gun back under the seat, put the car in reverse, and waved good-bye to my old friend the brook.

Was it just my imagination...or did my guardian angels breathe a sigh of relief as I headed into tomorrow?

Endnotes

1. Again, because of the intense, cataclysmic subject matter, *Follow the Yellow Brick Road* isn't appropriate reading for young children. PG—Parental discretion is advised. The language, authentic and graphic at points, was not written to be deliberately coarse or offensive. Actually, much of it has been toned down from the original R-rating.

2. "Tomorrow" by Martin Charnin and Charles Strose. Published by Warner Bros. and Edwin H. Morris. Used by permission.

3. Jer. 29:11.

4. "Tomorrow"

"Afraid"

Feather beds and patchwork quilts
Cower down
Hide inside the flannel gown
Hungry fire licks the log
Sneaking breathing makes a fog
Smell of sausage in the air
Stomach growling, do I dare
move and run to kitchen's shelter?
Aproned angel—I can't tell her
'bout the monster in the night
Hand on throat that squeezes tight
Innocence and trust betrayed
The demon has a name

"Afraid"[c]

Chapter 3

LIFE BEFORE OPRAH

What is it about holidays?

It was an unusually chilly Thanksgiving morning as I made a hasty barefooted trek from the backroom of my parents' home across the cold concrete of the double-car garage. I lifted the lid of the white enamel freezer, half stood on my head as I rummaged through butcher-wrapped pork chops, cans of orange juice, and plastic containers filled with butter beans.

Aha!

The hiding bags of homegrown corn on the cob!

Just as I turned to dash back to the awaiting warmth and soothing aromas of Mother's holiday cooking, I was startled to see my father standing there. In all the commotion, I hadn't heard him walk in. A strained, troubled expression racked his ashen face. He nervously jingled loose change in the pocket of his blue jeans.

"Honey, there's something I need to ask you and I hardly know how to begin," he said, staring down at his shuffling feet.

Oh no, what was it now? Could it be something else about my divorce? Was some juicy, new rumor circulating?

After all these months, I just wanted to relax and enjoy a peaceful family time this Thanksgiving without re-hashing all my failures.

Dad appeared much older than his normal youthful self. Whatever was troubling him was serious and obviously painful for him to talk about. Maybe it wasn't about me after all.

He cleared his throat and began. "Honey, one of your cousins told her father that John Doe[1] sexually abused her throughout her childhood. She says she wasn't the only one."

I froze in terror.

"Your uncle has asked all the boys to find out from their daughters if John did it to them, too."

Hot tears of panic spilled down my cheeks. A lump in my throat choked back the words. I was paralyzed by the dread of finally admitting the thing I feared most. After an excruciatingly long moment, I simply nodded, "Yes."

Unearthly silence hung in the air as we both stared awkwardly at his feet. My dad, who seldom cries, sniffled and quietly rubbed away the tears streaking his anguished face.

"Buck, long distance!" Mother beckoned from her busy kitchen.

We both jumped. Startled back into earth time. Disoriented and uncertain what to do next. With an apologetic hug, Dad turned and trudged with heavy steps back into the house. I don't know how long I stood there, my heart as glacial as the icy bags of corn clinging to my now-numb fingers. After all those years of trying to forget the horrible secrets behind closed doors, it was almost inconceivable that my precious dad would be the first person to open my double-locked Pandora's box.

What am I supposed to do now? O God! Are they going to make me confront John?

"Everybody will think it was all your fault," Accusation slithered. "When he denies it, *you* will look like the malicious liar."

Accusation's deadly cohort chimed in.

"You could have tried harder to stop him, but you didn't," Shame sneered. "What if the pressure of a few little indiscretions being exposed causes John to have a heart attack and die?"

I instinctively clapped one hand over my mouth to stifle a wrenching sob. Acid bile mingled with the salty taste of blood as I unconsciously bit my lower lip.

"Why didn't you just deny it ever happened to you?" Liar hissed. "How can you forget all the other times he was wonderful to you? You don't have to make him out to be such a monster!"

"What will people think of you now?" probed Fear. "Before it's all over, *YOU* will be the villain."

I was tumbling headlong down a jagged mountainside towards the black abyss called Hopelessness, about to be buried alive by the avalanche of netherworld voices, when the rope of Truth dropped into my battered heart.

God is faithful; He will not let you be tempted beyond what you can bear...He will also provide a way out so that you can stand up under it (1 Corinthians 10:13b NIV).

"Reba Faye, did you have to go to Siberia to get that corn?" Mother summoned. I hurriedly wiped my nose on my favorite sweatshirt (I never seem to have a *Kleenex* when I need one) and put on my "I'm-okay-I-just-stubbed-my-toe" face to account for my tears.

I am always amazed how The Voice can rise just one decibel above all other voices.

I heard Him.

And once more, Truth was just enough to cling to.

⸱◡ ◡⸱

*R*emember life before Oprah?

Remember life before tell-all TV talk shows educated viewers?

Remember when family secrets really were secret? Before our vocabularies included phrases like "good touch/bad touch"...before *dysfunctional, co-dependent* and *enabling* were popular buzzwords?

Remember when sexually abused children each thought they were the only one living such a horrible nightmare?

Do you ever feel at risk when your private world is being invaded? Are you threatened when your most intimate secrets are about to be exposed?

In Mark 4:22-23, Jesus teaches about secrets:

There is nothing hidden which will not be revealed, nor has anything been kept secret but that it should come to light. If anyone has ears to hear, let him hear (NKJV).

We're not keeping secrets, we're telling them; we're not hiding things, we're bringing them out into the

open. Are you listening to this? Really listening?
(TM)

Good Secrets/Bad Secrets

*L*et's make it clear: there are good secrets and bad secrets.

A perfect example of a "good secret" is Esther 2:10 when Esther's wise cousin, Mordecai, charged her not to divulge her true identity. Esther's survival and the fate of an entire nation depended upon her ability to keep the secret until God's time for it to be revealed.

A classic example of a "bad secret" is when King David had an adulterous affair with Bathsheba and arranged for her husband's murder. In Second Samuel 12:12, Nathan the prophet confronts David with his sin: "You did it secretly."

Often we think there is a gray area concerning bad secrets, especially if we weren't the one at fault. For instance, if we were molested or abused as a child, there is a tendency to hide or pretend it didn't really happen. Sometimes the pain is too much to bear, so we slip into denial. Or we "take an aspirin" and hope the pain will go away.

Out of love, God lifts up the rug and shines the light of revelation on the dirt we've tried so diligently to conceal. He reveals our private hurts to bring us out and release us from our guilt and shame.

If we run from the Light, He has a way of burning a hole in the carpet!

In Genesis 3, we read the story of Adam and Eve hiding from God because they didn't want Him to see their nakedness. God didn't ask, *"Where are you?"* or *"What have you done?"* because He didn't know.

He's God—He knows everything.

He was offering Adam and Eve the opportunity to come clean...immediately.

——— ·◡ ◡· ———

GOLDEN STEPPING STONE
Don't sweep your dirt under the carpet.
Let God clean it up!

——— ·◡ ◡· ———

Why did God shine light on their sinful acts?

- To encourage them to deal swiftly with the issues
- To provoke an admission of their disobedience
- To prompt their confession
- To cause them to ask for and receive forgiveness without delay
- To draw them back into right standing and unbroken fellowship with Him

That's still God's plan and pattern for His children today. But Adam and Eve refused His loving hand reaching to lift them from their sin. Instead, they began to accuse the serpent, God, and each other. Their pitiful attempt to cover their sin with fig leaves was woefully inadequate. God sovereignly and mercifully intervened. He established *the principle of atonement* by slaying an animal and covering Adam and Eve—and their sins—with garments of blood-soaked skins.

Through the sacrifice and shed blood of God's Son, our sins are atoned for—both now and forevermore. When we confess and forsake our sin—repent and turn back to

God—we are cleansed and covered with forgiveness. Our sins are gone!

Endnotes

1. A man whose real name shall remain anonymous. In an effort to respect individuals' right to privacy and protect identities, I have changed some names and blended some stories in this book.

No one takes pleasure
in opening up festering wounds
or seeing loved ones squirm
under a microscope.

So what happens?

The pain perseveres
and the infection spreads
until we are emotionally
or physically diseased
or incapacitated.

Chapter 4

SKELETONS IN THE CLOSET

What is it about secrets?

*W*ill Rogers once said, "Live so that you could sell the family parrot to the town gossip." Most of us would rather kill the bird.

Let's face it: every family is dysfunctional to some extent. In layman's terms, *dysfunctional* simply means something is not functioning the way it was originally intended. (In hillbilly-eze..."It jest ain't workin' right.")

And every family has deep, dark secrets.

Why do we persist in concealing issues which only serve to debilitate and cripple us?

Our reasons are innumerable; our excuses are endless.

PRIDE. *"This is who we are...this is how we've always been. What's wrong with that?"*

The family's identity is forged from an attitude of arrogance, smugness, superiority, or unwillingness to change.

31

God can't stomach arrogance or pretense; believe me, He'll put those upstarts in their place (Proverbs 16:5 TM).

"The pride of your heart [has] deceived you, you who live in the clefts of the rocks, who occupy the heights of the hill. Though you build your nest as high as the eagle's, from there I will bring you down," declares the Lord (Jeremiah 49:16b NIV).

PERPETUATION. *"What would people think if they found out how we really are?"*

Many families hide behind elaborate façades to maintain the respectability of their family name or some perceived image of credibility.

Our ancestors are dead and buried, and everything's going on just as it has from the first day of creation. Nothing's changed (2 Peter 3:4 TM).

PROTECTION. *"I don't know if Grandpa (or Mama or Timmy or whoever) could handle the truth. We've got to protect them."*

By camouflaging and shielding our loved ones, we often compound the problems.

You shall know the truth, and the truth shall make you free (John 8:32 NKJV).

PANIC AND PARALYSIS. *"I'm scared to death...if we start pulling on a thread, our whole family may unravel."*

Families are shrouded in secrecy through fears of all kinds: fear of detection, fear of punishment, fear of separation, fear of increased abuse, fear of loss, fear of not being believed...and the list goes on.

Fear is crippling...Fear involves torment (1 John 4:18 TM/NKJV).

PROCRASTINATION. *"If things get really bad, maybe we'll deal with it then. We just aren't ready yet..."*

We avoid or postpone facing painful issues, trying not to upset the apple cart or hoping for some eleventh-hour miracle. Or we feel as though confrontation will only make matters worse. Granted, timing is crucial, but most of us just don't want to go there—period.

The "right time" is now, and the "day of salvation" is now. (2 Corinthians 6:2b NCV).

PAIN. *"It's too painful. It hurts too bad..."*

No one takes pleasure in opening up festering wounds or seeing loved ones squirm under a microscope. So what happens? The pain perseveres and the infection spreads until we are emotionally and/or physically diseased and/or incapacitated. Listen to Jeremiah's lament:

Why is my pain perpetual and my wound incurable, refusing to be healed?....Therefore thus says the Lord [to Jeremiah]: If you return [and give up this mistaken tone of distrust and despair], then I will give you again a settled place of quiet and safety, and you will be My minister; and if you separate the precious from the vile [cleansing your own heart from unworthy and unwarranted suspicions concerning God's faithfulness], you shall be My mouthpiece (Jeremiah 15:18-19a).

PERVERTED PERCEPTION. *"If God really loved us, He wouldn't have let this happen."*

Blaming and accusing God is older than Adam. When our thinking becomes perverted, our focus shifts from the real problem. Identify your real enemy—and it's not God.

> *Be careful! Watch out for attacks from the devil, your great enemy. He prowls around like a roaring lion, looking for some victim to devour. Take a firm stand against him, and be strong in your faith* (1 Peter 5:8-9a NLT).

> [Jesus said] *"The thief does not come except to steal, and to kill, and to destroy. I have come that they may have life, and that they may have it more abundantly"* (John 10:10 NKJV).

Is Silence Golden?

*I*n the epic story *Exodus* by Leon Uris, a group of European Jewish orphans escape from Hitler's Holocaust to a Palestinian kibbutz with the help of Ari ben Canaan and Kitty Fremont. Once in Palestine, their young lives are again threatened during an Arab uprising and they are forced to evacuate the kibbutz for a safer location. The only route to safety passes by a hostile Arab military camp.

Ari and Kitty determine the best time for the dangerous escape is the middle of the night under the cloak of darkness when the babies would be sleeping and their covert activities would go undetected by the enemy.

Just one innocent cry piercing the moonless night and their whole plan would be thwarted. In one of the most dramatic, heartrending moments of the story, Ari and Kitty devise a plan to ensure the children's absolute silence: *they affix strips of heavy tape over the delicate mouth of each child.*

There is a time to keep silence. Sometimes the preservation of life depends on it.

However, many family members hold others hostage, threatening physical abuse, emotional torment, loss of love and even death if the deep dark secrets from behind closed doors are divulged.

"...if you ever tell anyone, I'll kill you!"

*A*nne told me her sad story of emotional and sexual abuse when she was a middle-aged woman. As she finally felt free to share with me, God began to heal and restore her.

Anne's saga began when she was an innocent four-year-old. Although she protested and voiced her intention to tell her parents, Grandfather menaced, *"You're just a stupid, little kid. Your parents will never believe you over me....If you ever tell anyone, I'll kill you!"*

Grandfather effectively "taped Anne's mouth shut" by his continual intimidation and convincing threats. In her twenties when Grandfather died, she nevertheless felt his hand reaching out from the grave, still silencing her.

After all, wasn't he a revered, beloved patriarch?

How could she betray his memory by disclosing the horrible truth?

While she couldn't bypass the process of admitting the trauma and abuse and then be willing to forgive her grandfather for his atrocities against her, I saw God do for her what she had never been able to do for herself.

One night we were worshiping together in a revival service. The presence of God was thick, intense, and awesome. I glanced down to the altar at Anne, the glow of newfound freedom emanating from her face. Hands uplifted in praise, she wept and laughed at the same time as the Lord probed her heart and uprooted the residual effects of her traumatic childhood. She reminded me of a little girl worshiping her Father uninhibited, unrestricted.

The next day, Anne told me what had happened to her at the altar.

"Reba, the Lord did something incredible for me! He totally changed my perspective of my grandfather. Even though I've gone through counseling in my twenties and the Lord has taken away the anger and bitterness over my grandfather, I was still influenced by him.

"When someone mentioned him in passing...a sudden, unexpected twinge of pain made me catch my breath. I would flash back to the first time he molested me when I was four years old. I relived the horrifying images of us sitting on the hunter green sofa watching TV...the nauseating scent of his aftershave and smoker's breath...that familiar terror growing in my gut. No one else may have noticed, but I was still affected.

"Last night in the presence of God, I saw Grandfather and me sitting on the same hunter green sofa. Only this time, I was an adult. We were sitting on either end of the sofa, talking, laughing and enjoying the normal, loving relationship grandfathers and granddaughters are supposed to have.

"The Lord said, 'See, Anne. I have given you a new picture.' "

Now when Anne thinks of her grandfather, she smiles at *the new picture* without dredging up old, hurtful images.

I absolutely love watching the Lord sovereignly take the teeth out of the devil's bite! I rejoice every time He defeats death in someone like Anne and resurrects hope, trust, and peace of mind.

> *O death, where is your sting? O* [grave], *where is your victory?* (1 Corinthians 15:55 NKJV)

———— ·୨ ୧· ————

GOLDEN STEPPING STONE
*Let the Painter transform
your old, hurtful images
into new, healed pictures.*

———— ·୨ ୧· ————

The Answer Is 49

Our God is a God of restoration. A simple definition of *restore* is "to put back into its original, intended condition." Only God can restore and make lives new. I don't know how He does it, but that's okay. He's God—and I'm not. (See Isaiah 55:8-9.)

Our wonderfully eccentric friend, Pastor Buzzy Sutherland, was born and raised in the backwoods of Arkansas. Brother Buzzy is a brilliant Bible scholar with incredible revelation of God's Word. His masterpiece sermons are spiced with charming Southern one-liners. I think he has a double doctorate in "hillbilly-eze."

He once told me, "When I was up there at that school, they tried everything they knew to teach me that there algebra. That teacher told me *xyz=49* and told me to go figure it out. I said, 'Why am I worried how to get *xyz* if

I've got the 49? When you got the answer, who cares how you got there...' "

Brother Buzzy's right. Many times I don't have to know the *xyz* of how God does what He does. I'm just thrilled to have the 49.

Motives of the Heart

*W*hile it is crucial to deal with the dirt under our "family rugs," that doesn't necessarily mean we have to expose it for the whole world to see. It is imperative to search our hearts: *"What is our motive for telling others?"*

There is a fine line between repenting and repairing... and perpetuating and prolonging the effects of the dirt. Most pastors or seasoned counselors have dealt with people like Jill who claimed to have forgiven her adulterous ex-husband, Gilbert. She read Scriptures such as, "Vengeance is Mine, I will repay," says the Lord (Rom. 12:19b NKJV) and experienced a twisted sense of satisfaction.

"Even though I won't be the one to get him, at least I know he didn't get away with it!"

When Gilbert's secretary-turned-lover dumped him, Jill gloated and gave glory to God "for making him pay." That's not forgiveness as Jesus modeled.

———— •‿ ‿• ————

GOLDEN STEPPING STONE
Confrontation leads us to negotiation
which leads us to reconciliation.

———— •‿ ‿• ————

You know you have truly forgiven when you can pray "God, have mercy on them. Don't give them what they deserve."

Jesus demonstrated this highest form of forgiveness as He hung on the cross and beseeched the Father on behalf of His betrayers and murderers.

> *"Father, forgive them for they know not what they do"* (Luke 23:34 KJV).

In other words, *"They may be killing Me, but don't punish them for it."*

Where Do We Start?

*I*n approaching fragile family issues and healing deep wounds, the ultimate goal of any confrontation must be reconciliation. There are three parts to the equation: confrontation, negotiation and reconciliation. Confrontation leads us to negotiation...and negotiation leads us to reconciliation.

We must be willing to handle these difficult issues—and each other—with utmost wisdom and love. We need to ask ourselves some hard questions:

- What are we trying to accomplish?
- When is the right timing?
- Who in the family needs to be involved?
- Will innocent people be hurt by knowing?
- How much do we need to tell young children?
- Are we going to keep this within the family?
- Do we need to enlist the help of a neutral third party?
- What is our plan for forgiving, healing and reconciling?

Whirlwinds
have a way of picking you up
then crashing you down
into a strange land
that sure ain't Kansas,
Dorothy.

Chapter 5

THE WIND BEGAN TO SWITCH...

‑ 1981 ‑

What is it about bathrooms?

You know you're in trouble when you discover a half-empty bottle of Stolichnaya vodka stashed in the cool reservoir of your commode.

All the blood rushed to my face and blue toilet bowl disinfectant drizzled down my jeans as I sank onto the cold bathroom tiles, overwhelmed by a wave of nausea. Blistering tears erupted from the cauldron of emotions brewing inside.

"Maybe you're not so crazy after all," Consolation cooed. "Now you know the real reason this schizophrenic relationship is like being married to Dr. Jekyl and Mr. Hyde."

The first few months of marriage to Dony had been a wild roller coaster ride. What began as simple friendship and songwriting partnership gradually developed into remarkable chemistry. I was attracted to Dony's charismatic, fun-loving personality and obvious creative genius. He was handsome, spontaneous, unpredictable...and dangerous. He resurrected my shattered self-esteem and almost convinced me I was beautiful even when I wore faded blue jeans and very little make-up. Dony seemed to love me for *me* and not just as some Barbie Doll singer.

The Gift

*D*ony was a package deal. He came complete with a beautiful little daughter from his first marriage. Dionne had a wonderful mother—even Dony admitted that—so I knew his adorable, freckle-faced "half-pint" (as he lovingly called her) would only be with us every other weekend.

By that point, doctors had already warned me that I would probably never bear children. It was risky enough for me to give myself to Dony. I certainly couldn't gamble getting too close to Dionne, so I determined to love her from a distance. Consequently, I got out my brick and mortar and proceeded to build thick walls to protect my heart. At the same time, I always looked forward to our weekends with this charming, smart, precocious, inquisitive, beautiful bundle of energy.

Late one Friday night, I went into her room to check on her. In spite of my self-defense attempts to suppress any maternal instincts, I had to make sure she was still breathing.

Boy, does she look like her daddy! Same cheekbones. Same mischievous eyes. Same pudgy fingers. Same shaped toes. Same curled-up corners of the mouth.

Her blankets kicked off, she lay sideways on the bed, a favorite stuffed toy clutched under one arm and...

What's that in her other hand? Oh. A now-withered dandelion she thought especially pretty.

Earlier that afternoon during our family walk in the park, Dionne had picked a handful of colorful wildflowers with a few anonymous weeds thrown in. She had planned to take them home to her mother. In a futile attempt to preserve her "bouquet," we had stuck them in a jelly jar vase on her nightstand.

I eased the bedraggled, smelly, wilted weed through her green and yellow stained fingers. She stirred, stretched lazily and peered up at me through thick eyelashes. With a sleepy smile, she yawned, "I love you, Mama Reba."

I was a goner.

With one simple sentence, she had weaseled her way under my Fort Knox walls straight into my heart.

I never meant to love her so much.

The Whirlwind

New marriage.

New husband.

New daughter.

New start?

I surrendered to the whirlwind of impulsive abandonment. But whirlwinds have a way of picking you up—then crashing you down into a strange land that sure ain't Kansas, Dorothy.

Drug and alcohol addiction takes no prisoners. "Divorced Miss Gospel Singer" had gone and married a closet addict.

I never knew what to expect from Dony. His extreme passionate highs were followed by deep depression lows and inexplicable withdrawal. One moment he would surprise me with an impromptu romantic picnic in front of a

43

crackling fireplace, making me feel cherished and desirable. The next moment his erratic outbursts of unprovoked jealousy, violence, and sadistic mind games evoked terror, panic, and incredulity.

"You failed with your first marriage...now here you go again," chided Condemnation.

Absentmindedly biting the fleshy part of my forefinger, I stifled a wrenching sob.

Dear God...could it be my fault?

"You're just a good-for-nothing wife," frowned Disgrace. "You'll never make any man happy."

The high Victorian ceiling caved in, sucking the life out of the tiny bathroom as Fear droned a singsong chant.

Second verse same as the first
Another marriage in a hearse[1]

A merry-go-round of contorted images twirled hypnotically and willed me like Scrooge to watch tragic scenes of my life.

Reba Past: divorce, rejection, guilt, and shame.

An eerily out-of-tune pipe organ crescendoed with nightmarish gallops, the giddy melody prancing loudly across a mournful dirge.

Reba Present: new marriage, new rejection, new guilt, and new shame.

Gyrating out of control, the runaway carousel screeched with frenzied mockery.

The wind began to switch
The house to pitch

44

And suddenly the hinges
Started to unhitch[2]

Reba Future: no love, no music, no hope, no me.

On the verge of hysteria, oxygen-starved lungs rasped within my heaving chest. I shivered more from horror than from the chill of the bathroom tiles. Teetering on the edge of despair, I blindly felt for the wall. Something real to quell the dizzying tornado. Something solid to regain my fading equilibrium. My fingers brailed their way up the grass-cloth wallpaper in search of the brass towel ring. I seized a monogrammed terrycloth lifeline and slowly struggled to stand.

Still wobbly, I collided with a framed picture and sent it toppling precariously to the floor. Staring back at me through broken glass was a faded black-and-white photo of little Dony surrounded by his four brothers. I guardedly picked up the familiar picture of The McGuire Brothers clad in matching suits, starched shirts, and bow ties.

The McGuire Brothers

Raised in a preacher's home, the musically gifted McGuire boys had created quite a stir in churches throughout the Bible belt. Fifteen-year-old Robert played guitar and was a fiery preacher. Jack David, age 13, thumped a mean bass. Jerry, at age 11, plucked steel guitar, but he was a real star who thrilled congregations when he dramatically "walked the aisles" and belted out "At the Roll Call." Adorable nine-year-old twins, Dony and Ronnie, completed the dynamic Gospel group, with Ronnie squeezing the accordion and Dony burning up the piano. The McGuire Brothers' boyish good looks, musical talents, and unique family blend of harmonies charmed fans everywhere.

From time to time, older sisters, Wilma and Brenda, joined the boys in their concerts.

My eyes were automatically drawn to Dony's compelling presence in the photograph. He looked so cute and cuddly, so innocent and proud, in his Sunday best. When I fell in love with him, I always said I wanted to have a son just like him.

Now I wasn't so sure.

"How could anyone who looks so sweet turn into the devil in disguise?" I sighed.

"A trap was set for him long ago," the Voice announced. *"The enemy has tried repeatedly to destroy Dony's life. Remember the accident?"*

How many times had Mom McGuire recounted the details of that fateful day?

Endnotes

1. "Marriage Dirge" by Reba Rambo-McGuire and Judy A. Gossett. 2001 Rambo-McGuire Publishing. Used by permission.

2. "It Really Was No Miracle" by E.Y. "Yip" Harburg. Published by MGM. 1938. Used by permission.

If you do your part,
God will do His.

Chapter 6

TRAGEDY STRIKES

⁓ 1961 ⁓

What is it about Sundays?

It was an overcast yet unusually warm day in February. Mac and Mabel McGuire's family had been invited over after Sunday service to share a leisurely lunch at the home of fellow church members, the Eatons. All the kids played outside and the men folk pitched horseshoes, while the mothers put finishing touches on mountains of Southern fried chicken, mashed potatoes and brown gravy, green beans and smoked ham hocks, fried okra, and homemade peach cobbler. The sweet aroma of Mom McGuire's famous yeast rolls rising to perfection in the oven wafted through the screen door.

Boy! They were gonna feast today!

⁓

*L*ive wire nine-year-old Dony just had to get in a quick ride on the neighbor's shiny red Western Flyer bicycle. He jumped on the bike and flew down the hill, entering the curb lane of the highway where a mud-splattered, semi-trailer truck was parked just above the driveway. The driver of a northbound automobile swerved around the truck and steered back into her lane when she suddenly caught a glimpse of Dony.

But it was too late!

In a panic, she jerked the steering wheel and stomped on the brakes, sending the car into a smoky, black skid. Spinning wildly out of control, the steel rear bumper caught Dony's leg. With a hideous, unearthly pop, his left foot was ripped off as his little body catapulted 20 feet into the air and slammed in a crumpled heap into the oncoming traffic.

Still conscious, Dony could hear tires screeching to avoid hitting him.

Big brother Robert was the first to weave his way through the cars to where his baby brother lay in shock.

Unaware he had lost his foot, Dony tried to jump up and get off the dangerous highway. Every time he tried to take another step, he fell face first on the rough asphalt until a sobbing Robert scooped him up and carried him to the safety of the roadside.

Inebriated, the driver shrieked hysterically, "It wasn't my fault! I didn't do it!" until a burly truck driver angrily shoved her toward the horrifying evidence dangling on her bloodied bumper.

"Mama, Why Can't I Walk?"

*D*ony's parents, brothers, sister Wilma, and her husband, Herb, heard the crash and rushed to the scene of the accident. They knelt around

Dony, crying loudly, begging God to spare him as his life's blood spilled onto the graveled roadside.

Mom carefully drew Dony's mangled body into her lap and held him close. She lifted his twisted left arm, broken bones jutting through the gored flesh, and laid it gently across his chest.

"Mama, is my foot cut off?"

"Honey, you're gonna be just fine," Mom wept, wiping his face with the corner of her blood-soaked apron. "Somebody run and get the pastor."

"Brother Eaton, did anybody call an ambulance?" Dad McGuire pressed, his voice betraying his alarm.

"I did, Mac," replied Brother Eaton. "They'll be here shortly."

Delirious from loss of blood, Dony asked weakly, "Mama, why can't I walk? Is my foot gone?"

"Don't you worry, baby. The Lord's got everything under control," Mom reassured. "Where's the pastor?"

Pastor North ran breathlessly through the crowd and knelt between Mom and Dad McGuire.

"Dear God!" he gasped in disbelief. The accident was much worse than he anticipated. This family really needed the Lord's help. Instinctively, the faithful pastor started to pray.

"Dony keeps asking me if his foot was cut off," Mom whispered in hushed, aching tones to Pastor North. Fear and helplessness filled her eyes. "What should I say?"

"Sister McGuire, you should just go on and tell him the truth," Pastor North spoke calmly. "You all need to be the ones to let him know."

"Mama, is my foot gone?" Dony slurred.

She looked questioningly into Dad's anguished eyes, drawing strength for her impossible task. Lovingly, he

51

placed his hand on her shoulder and simply nodded, "Go ahead."

Mom swallowed hard, sighed deeply and languished, "Yes, baby, your foot has been cut off."

When the ambulance arrived, Dony was slipping further into shock and losing massive amounts of blood. The attendants worked feverishly to stabilize him, then they strapped him onto a gurney and carefully lifted him into the ambulance.

"We'll be taking him to St. John's Hospital," the driver announced. "Parents can ride with us if you'd like."

"Don't worry about the boys," Wilma assured, already gathering the kids. "Herb and I will take them home with us."

Mom and Dad stepped up into the ambulance and sat down on either side of Dony. Dad lay across his son's broken little body, sobbing. Lifting up his father's head, Dony consoled, "It's gonna be alright, Daddy."

The Weight of Waiting

A skilled medical team struggled to keep Dony alive. Inevitably, surgeons were called in to amputate his left leg just below the knee as the tearful family and friends nervously paced the halls or quietly prayed in the waiting room.

"Why doesn't somebody tell us something?" Dad McGuire moaned, his voice riddled with frustration and anxiety. "It's been forever!"

"Now Mac, you need to calm down, honey," Mabel soothed as she moved yesterday's newspaper out of the only overstuffed chair in the airless waiting room and eased Mac down.

Everyone's nerves were frazzled. The strain of the last few hours was taking its toll when the operating room doors flung open and out strode a striking surgeon garbed in green scrubs. As he removed his surgical mask and cap, revealing a boyish smile and crew cut, he was humming "There's Power in the Blood."

"Mr. and Mrs. McGuire?" he scanned the waiting room. "Your son is still alive. He made it through the leg amputation as well as could be expected."

Mom stifled a sob of relief.

"It's okay, Mrs. McGuire. You've all been through a lot today. But you've got a very strong boy in there."

⤳ ⤺

*D*r. Jack Oldhouse was a born-again believer and a brilliant surgeon. His confidence and demeanor had an immediate calming effect on the family and friends gathered.

"Let me be frank with you. Your son isn't out of the woods yet," he continued. "Not only are there many serious internal injuries, we are very concerned about his left arm."

He guided the McGuires into a nearby lab, switched on the x-ray viewing lights and pointed to the shadows and skeletal images on Dony's x-rays.

"Here's what we're dealing with. In layman's terms, there are 13 breaks between the left wrist and elbow. His shoulder was mangled like hamburger meat," he patiently explained, tracing the gruesome films. "Notice how the left socket looks like crushed powder. The nerve and muscle damage is so severe...*if your son survives*...which we're all praying and hoping for...his arm might never grow or function properly. We may be faced with amputation of the left arm also."

Dr. Oldhouse was all too familiar with the inevitable stunned silence. "I'm so sorry. I know this isn't what you wanted to hear."

He quietly shepherded Mom and Dad McGuire back to the waiting room.

"I don't mean to pressure you, but we're going to need your decision right away. I'll give you a moment to talk it over..."

He turned to walk down the corridor and Mom McGuire followed.

"Doctor, when Dony was five years old, God promised me he would be a great piano player. Now...I've never heard of a good one-armed piano player, have you?"

Impressed by her obvious faith, the doctor shook his head. "Alright, Mrs. McGuire. I'll cast it, but there's so much injury and swelling, we may have to change the cast every day...and that can be very painful."

He lightly touched Mom's shoulder. "You know I'm believing God along with you, but we've got to face the fact that even a cast won't repair nerve damage."

"Doctor, if you do your part," Mom replied with quiet confidence, "God will do His."

The Trap

The drug administered to Dony for his multiple surgeries was ether, probably one of the cruelest drugs when a patient is coming out from under its influence. Dony threw up every few minutes, then experienced hours of dry heaves. His body was so racked with endless retching, he felt like every suture and incision would rip apart.

Unconsciousness was a blessed relief.

Thankfully, Dony did survive. But during the next six weeks, he screamed incessantly from excruciating agony.

Writhing wildly with phantom pain, he insisted, "My leg can't be gone! I can feel my foot! It's killing me!"

Morphine was injected every three hours—to medicate and appease his torment. Every time the dressing on his leg was changed, he was given additional high-powered drugs.[1]

Mom was right about Dony's arm. Six weeks later, the doctors removed the original cast and marveled that his left arm functioned as perfectly as his right.[2] It was a certifiable miracle!

The McGuires knew Dony was going to be all right because he still had a silly sense of humor.

Recovering from leg amputation at St. John's, he was attended by Catholic nuns wearing black and white habits. He thought it was funny to drop things and make a mess on the floor just so the nuns would have to bend over and pick them up. He stuck out his heavy plaster cast and the nuns inevitably banged their heads against it when they stood up, sending him into gales of laughter.

Eventually, he was discharged from the hospital in record time. (His mother thought his orneriness might have had something to do with the early release.) Dony returned home to his grateful family, armed with an arsenal of pain pills.

Two Steps Forward, Three Steps Back

"*D*ony's leg is healing, but it will be at least six months before he's ready to learn to walk again," Dr. Oldhouse predicted.

But the brothers didn't accept that gloomy prognosis. They refused to let Dony sit around feeling sorry for himself. Instead they all pitched in and taught him to walk again. Within 90 days, he was fitted for his first artificial limb.

The prosthesis was made out of soft balsam wood, literally whittled with precision knives by skilled craftsman, Clifford Cleggette, C.P. Crude by today's standards, Dony's first artificial limb had metal braces on the sides and hinges at the knee. It was then strapped to his thigh by a bulky leather corset attached to a belt around his waist which supported the weight of the limb when he walked.

Soon Dony was back playing competitive sports.

But kids grow—and so do their limbs. Throughout his adolescent and teen years, doctors performed multiple surgeries on Dony's left leg, trimming back the bones and flesh to the most appropriate length to fit into each new prosthesis. With each operation, increased dosages of high-powered drugs were administered to help control the pain...and to satisfy his growing drug dependence.

The second surgery, he shared a room with another amputee who cried all the time. Dony asked for drugs just to escape from the incessant crying. He wondered why the poor boy didn't just relax and enjoy the drugs.

Dony knew if he threw a big enough fit, the nursing staff would give him more drugs. Needless to say, he threw a lot of fits.

Those first few years birthed his craving. He quickly learned to enjoy the euphoria. Even when the pain was bearable, he discovered if he yelled loud enough and long enough, some well-meaning but misguided nurse would help send him to la-la land. By his final surgery at age 15, he was a full-fledged addict.

The Tornado

Dony's prodigious musical genius was obvious and by age 16, he had been handpicked to play piano for several prominent Southern Gospel groups. On the road with one group in particular that indulged in all manner of ungodly behavior, Dony started drinking wine and beer.

By age 20, he discovered Nyquil somewhat by accident when he had a particularly bad cold and cough. Someone suggested the popular cold remedy with high alcohol content. Dony was coughing a lot, so he just chugalugged most of the bottle and climbed into his bunk on the touring bus, thinking, "What an incredible buzz." From that point on, Dony kept a bottle of Nyquil in his bag.

Guess that cold must have lasted for years.

Not long after, a so-called "good friend" introduced him to hard liquor. By age 22, he smoked his first of many marijuana joints. He also had a pack-a-day cigarette habit.

His "good friend" showed him how to go to different doctors around the country and obtain multiple prescriptions of uppers and downers. Soon Dony was turning on to cocaine and other illegal drugs, dangerously mixing them with alcohol.

By the time Dony and I met and married, he was a full-blown alcoholic and drug addict...and I was an unsuspecting fool who didn't know the difference.

Endnotes

1. Until recently, doctors didn't fully understand the nature of addiction. Today they would have offered less intrusive treatments and followed up the many subsequent surgeries with counseling. But back in the early 1960s, they were inadvertently turning an innocent nine-year-old into a chemically dependent addict.

2. The doctors were amazed when they read the ambulance report and discovered Mom McGuire had placed Dony's badly broken arm across his chest in the exact position for it to be set properly.

Unresolved shame
is the breeding ground for perversion.
Unresolved shame
creates a distorted image
of love and intimacy.
Typically, this false perception
spawns abuse—abnormal use.
Abuse is not just a female issue.

Chapter 7

GUILT AND SHAME

*I am tempted to continue telling my story; however,
the next couple of chapters deal with strategic subject matters I believe will help you. I urge you.
Whatever you do—don't miss them!*

What is it about twisted perceptions?

When the lens of our lives is out of focus, there
is a subtle blurring of the concepts of *guilt*
and *shame*. This chapter is not intended to be an author-
itative dissertation on such complex psychological issues;
however, it is vitally important to distinguish between
the two.

In *Tired of Trying to Measure Up*[1], author Jeff
VanVonderen says:

> "Shame is often confused with guilt. But they're
> not the same. God created you and me so that
> when we do something wrong we experience a
> sense of guilt. Guilt is like a spiritual nerve-
> response to sin, an emotion in response to

wrong behavior ("I acted in a way that was wrong, and I feel guilty"). Those uncomfortable impulses that stab our conscience are meant to turn us away from the wrong we're doing and turn us back to God. In that sense, *guilt is a healthy thing*. Because guilt comes as result of something you and I do, we can do something about it—change our behavior—and the guilty feeling will go away.

"Shame, on the other hand, is not just a feeling, though we often speak of it that way ('You ought to feel ashamed of yourself').

"*Shame is the belief or mindset that something is wrong with you.*

"It's something you can live with and not neces- sarily be aware of. It's not that you feel bad about your behavior, it's that you sense or believe you are deficient, defective or worthless as a human being.

"Consequently, you develop a shame-based way of looking at yourself. You accept the view that others might slip up and make mistakes once in a while, but they're still basically worthwhile people. You, however, are like a mirror image of that: No matter how many times you get it right (whatever it is, according to the standards of your environment) you will never be acceptable. Down deep, you believe something is wrong with you."

———— •ᴗ ᴖ• ————

GOLDEN STEPPING STONE
Guilt is a spiritual nerve-response to sin.
Guilt is a healthy thing.

———— •ᴗ ᴖ• ————

In layman's terms, this is *guilt*:

"I feel bad for having stolen a cookie from the cookie jar. I did wrong."

These are justified bad feelings of guilt meant to lead us to repentance.

But this is *shame*:

"The reason I stole the cookie is because I am a bad person."

These bad feelings reflect a sense of worthlessness that often prevents or postpones repentance and subsequent healing.

"Why would God want to hear from somebody like me?"

Here's another aspect of shame:

"Cookies are missing from the cookie jar. While I didn't take them, it still must be my fault they are gone."

The enemy compounds the sense of worthlessness with bogus insinuations, distorting rational and healthy thinking.

"When I'm around so-and-so, I feel guilty."

Did you do something wrong?

"No, but I still feel guilty. It must be my fault."

Guilt can be resolved through sincere repentance but shame keeps you at a distance from God because you feel dirty and defiled, worthless and weak, ruined and irreparable.

Power of Shame

Shame in others can ignite the smoldering embers of shame in you, especially if you have developed a pattern of succumbing to the unrealistic expectations and demands of others.

In his excellent book, *Changes That Heal*,[2] Dr. Henry Cloud demonstrates how shame breeds shame in this excerpt of a counseling session with a woman named Sandy. He begins:

"Why don't you just tell your mother that you don't want to come home for Thanksgiving? You're thirty years old. That's old enough to choose to spend a holiday with your friends," I said.

"But that would make her very angry," Sandy replied. "I could never do that. It's mean."

"How can you 'make' her angry? Why do you think you have that much power?" I asked.

"If I didn't go home for the holidays, that would make her mad. It's as simple as that."

"Then I guess you think you have the power to make her happy as well. Is that right?" I wondered aloud.

"Well, of course," Sandy replied. "If I do what she wants, I can make her happy."

"You're a very powerful woman," I said. "It must be frightening to have that much power. But, if you are that powerful, why don't you have the power to make yourself feel good?"

"I don't know the answer to that. That's why I came to see you. So you could make me feel better."

"Oh, I see. Making your mother feel good makes you feel bad. Then, you come to see me, and I'll make you feel good. What am I supposed to do if that makes me feel bad?" I asked. "Maybe I could call your mother, and she could make ME feel better."

"You're crazy," she said. "How's she gonna make YOU feel better?"

"I don't know," I answered. "But as long as everyone is responsible for everyone else's feelings, I'm sure she would try to find a way."

Imagine what it must feel like to live a life of being responsible for someone else's feelings and out of control of your own.

That's the power of shame.

If fully grown adults like Sandy struggle with shame, abuse, and manipulation tactics of others, imagine how difficult it is for a child. An innocent child who experiences sexual and other forms of abuse is not emotionally developed enough to distinguish between guilt and shame.

Here was my childhood dilemma:

"Why didn't I try harder to stop him? It must have been my fault."

"He's such a wonderful man. It must have been my fault."

"Why would I make him out to be such a monster? It must have been my fault."

GOLDEN STEPPING STONE
*Shame is the belief or mindset
that something is wrong with you.*

The Root of Shame

The Lord opened my eyes to the diabolical origin of shame when I looked up the definitions of shame in *Vine's Complete Expository Dictionary of Old and New Testament Words.*

Bo'set: "shame; shameful thing..."...This word represents both shame and worthlessness. This word means a "shameful thing" as a substitute for the name *Baal.*[3]

Baal? What does Baal have to do with shame? I was amazed by these Biblical definitions of *Baal.*[4]

Ba'al: "master; baal...The primary meaning of *ba'al* is 'possessor'...a secondary meaning, 'husband' is clearly indicated by the phrase *ba'al has-issah* (literally, 'owner of the woman'). Thirdly, the word *ba'al* may denote any deity other than the God of Israel."

Can you see the inordinate correlation between shame and satan?

The name *Baal* is theologically interchangeable with the name *satan*. And according to *Vine's* definitions, *shame* can also be substituted for *Baal*.

This is the way satan uses shame. Something happens in our lives that opens the door to Baal/shame. Baal/shame institutes a stronghold of total worthlessness with the intention of becoming **master**, **possessor**, and **lord**.

Baal/shame becomes a god other than God Almighty. When Baal/shame establishes a throne in our hearts, he assumes legal authority and occupancy from which he rules and dictates our lives.

Baal/shame wants to marry himself to us (whether we are male or female)...to husband and master us.[5]

Thus, shame is far more powerful than guilt because it undermines and erodes the very foundation of life.

The seeds of shame sown in childhood can be carried for a lifetime unless you allow Holy Spirit to gently pluck them by the roots from the soil of your overcrowded heart.

The Fruit of Shame

Without going into all of the sordid details of the nightmare with my childhood abuser, John, the shame—disguised as guilt—became imprinted into my emotions and affected every area of my life for years.

After I was married, I experienced multiple miscarriages and subsequent corrective surgeries for endometriosis, fibroid tumors, twisted and blocked ovaries. Humiliating procedures, tests, and experimental medications only added to my sense of shame.

Something was wrong with me.

Did the sexual abuse mutilate me physically? No, but it deformed me psychologically and emotionally, eventually manifesting itself in my reproductive organs.

Remember: up to that point, I had not told anyone about the sexual abuse. Still, my insidious secret was betraying my physical body. My secret was killing me... literally.

I believe I was unable to carry a pregnancy through to full term because of the repeated experiences of sexual abuse in my childhood—the resulting, unending shame—and the fact that I had never dealt with it.

Fertility vs. Infertility

Take note: Old Testament history reveals that Baal was a common name given to the god of fertility in Canaan.[6]

If Baal/shame is the "god of fertility," could he also control and determine the reverse curse of infertility?

Remember: *Baal* and *shame* are interchangeable words. There are always parallels between the natural and supernatural realms.

In my heart of hearts, I *thought* I was worthless and undeserving of the joys of motherhood. Of course, shame's first cousin showed up.

"If you were to give birth to a daughter," Fear taunted, "the abuse would likely happen to her too."

As [a man] *thinketh in his heart, so is he* (Proverbs 23:7a KJV).

GOLDEN STEPPING STONE
*Shame is far more powerful than guilt
because it undermines and erodes
the very foundation of life.*

The Nature of Abuse

After ministering to thousands of women with various female and reproductive problems, I began to ask them, "Were you ever sexually or physically abused?"

Astonishingly, 99.9 percent have answered "yes."

I am not implying this statement constitutes a conclusive scientific study. This has been my personal experience in the laboratory of life...as a "minister/doctor" laboring in trauma centers called altars.

I am not suggesting that everyone who was abused becomes infertile or suffers reproductive problems; however, practically everyone I've ministered to who is infertile or suffering reproductive problems has been sexually, physically, or emotionally abused. Often they become emotionally, relationally, socially, or physically barren or impotent.

Recently while filming television shows with my friends Lindsay Roberts and Cheryl Pruitt-Salem, we began to compare notes. In our ministry to families, each of us discovered a definite link between abuse and reproductive problems.

What Is Abuse?

*I*n simple language, *abuse* means "abnormal use of." Anytime we are used for anything outside of God's intended purpose, that's abuse. And we know abuse leads to shame.

Some people are even ashamed of feeling shame. For example, they say, *"There was no penetration or real sexual contact."*

"I wasn't violated like some were, so why should I complain?"

"Other people have been through a lot worse than I have and have survived. I need to pull myself up by the bootstraps and go on..."

Shame is heaped upon shame.

I can never forget listening to a woman named Robin regurgitate her sad story of emotional abuse, sleep disorder, and infertility.

"When I was a little girl, my family was stationed as missionaries in a tropical Third World country. The intense heat and high humidity made sleep virtually impossible. As I lay in my tiny cubicle at night, almost without thinking, I threw off my sheets and nightgown to cool off and get relief from the suffocating heat and humidity. Eventually, I drifted off to sleep.

"Reba, have you ever woke up because you knew someone was watching you?

"I startled awake...only to find my father standing in the doorway, staring at my naked body with those glazed, hungry eyes. I'm not sure if he ever touched me...I don't remember...but my skin crawled as he gave me "that private look" throughout the day...when Mama was brushing my hair or bathing me in the galvanized tub. Even as I played with my favorite doll, I felt 'those eyes' undressing me."

Her father's mind games, the mental and emotional abuse—and the resulting shame—devastated Robin. When I met her, she was afraid of men and ministers, had very poor self-esteem, battled with a sleep disorder and suffered with unusually severe monthly periods and endometriosis. Robin was very bitter and confessed to hating the woman she had become.

As I gently walked her through the process of forgiveness, the Lord uncorked the bottled-up fear, anger, shame and mistrust. Baal/Shame was dethroned from Robin's life. What a joy to see her now...a healed, happily married woman with two beautiful children!

The Two Breeding Grounds

Our friend Pastor Rod Parsley powerfully preaches that "expectancy is the breeding ground for miracles." Throughout my life, I've discovered that expectant faith births miracles.

Conversely, unresolved shame is the breeding ground for perversion.

Unresolved shame creates a distorted image of love and intimacy. Typically, this false perception spawns abuse—abnormal use. It often leads its victims to becoming sexually under- or over-active.

You've got the "Ice Princess" mentality—exemplified by those who are afraid of sexual intimacy...and learn to go through the motions and put their minds somewhere else—in a safe place—as they did when they were children being abused.

The other extreme is the "Don Juan" mentality—the sexually promiscuous who believe hopping from bed to bed will satisfy their deep-seated longings for love and intimacy.

The nightmares of abuse don't just disappear as you grow older. I have held 80-year-old women...really, 80-year-old-little girls frozen in time...in my arms and wept with them as they finally revealed their hidden—but never forgotten—horror stories.

Abuse is not just a female issue. I have watched Dony embrace sobbing, brokenhearted men and teenagers who were abused and violated as young boys.

I never cease to be amazed as the Light of Glory begins to shine on the faces of people who have been released from chains of anguish and freed from torments of secrecy.

We strip Baal/shame of its destructive power over us whenever the deeds done in darkness are brought to the Light (see 1 Cor. 4:5). Whether you were the abuser or the "abusee," relief begins with confessing our dark deeds. This is the beginning of the healing, delivering process.

You have stripped off the old (unregenerate) self with its evil practices, and have clothed yourselves with the new [spiritual self], which is [ever in the process of being] renewed and remolded into [fuller and more perfect knowledge upon] knowledge after the image (the likeness) of Him Who created it (Colossians 3:9-10).

The Power of Perversion

*M*any victims of abuse have been deceived by Baal/shame, the god of fertility, and have sacrificed God's Genesis plan to be fruitful and multiply (see Gen. 1:28). In this alarming pattern, the seed of Baal/shame comes to full fruition and drives many men and women into homosexuality and lesbianism.

As in my previous references to infertility, let me underscore that not all abuse victims become homosexuals or lesbians. Many homosexuals were innocent victims of sexual abuse in their childhood while others have blatantly chosen that aberrant lifestyle. Many are mired in guilt, shame and condemnation while others have their consciences seared with a hot iron.

> *Some will turn away from the faith, giving attention to deluding and seducing spirits and doctrines that demons teach, through the hypocrisy and pretensions of liars whose consciences are seared (cauterized), who forbid people to marry...* (1 Timothy 4:1b-3a).

Notice the term *cauterized* or "seared with fire"...so that the conscience cannot be opened up again to the convicting, healing power of Holy Spirit.

The following passage of Romans 1:18, 21-32 is lengthy, but nonetheless essential in understanding the progression of perversion in homosexuality and lesbianism.

Let's look carefully at this pattern: sin, secrecy, wrong thinking, worshiping gods other than God Almighty, sexual impurity, shame, abuse, and consequences.

> *God's [holy] wrath and indignation are revealed from heaven against all ungodliness and unrighteousness of men* [sin] *who in their wickedness repress and hinder the truth* [secrecy] *and make it inoperative...because when they knew and recognized Him as God, they did not honor and glorify*

Him as God or give Him thanks. But instead they became futile and godless in their thinking [with vain imaginings, foolish reasoning, and stupid speculations] and their senseless minds were darkened [**wrong thinking**]. *Claiming to be wise, they became fools [professing to be smart, they made simpletons of themselves]. And by them the glory and majesty and excellence of the immortal God were exchanged for and represented by images, resembling mortal man and birds and beasts and reptiles. Therefore God gave them up in the lusts of their [own] hearts to sexual impurity, to the dishonoring of their bodies among themselves [abandoning them to the degrading power of sin]* [**sexual impurity**] *because they exchanged the truth of God for a lie and worshiped and served the creature rather than the Creator* [**worshiping gods other than God Almighty**]....*For this reason God gave them over and abandoned them to vile affections and degrading passions. For their women exchanged their natural function for an unnatural and abnormal one* [**abuse**], *and the men also turned from natural relations with women and were set ablaze (burning out, consumed) with lust for one another—men committing shameful acts with men* [**shame**] *and suffering in their own bodies and personalities the inevitable consequences and penalty of their wrongdoing and going astray* [**consequences**]...

Can you see the downward spiral of perversion?

Let's review the inevitable pattern: sin, secrecy, wrong thinking, worshiping gods other than God Almighty, sexual impurity, shame, abuse and consequences.

71

otice the term "shameful acts" in the last verse of
ssage. Baal/shame, the ancient god of fertility, is so
jealous that he wants nothing to be reproduced in
mankind except for himself...so he drives his victims to
propagate and infest others with himself—for himself.

Outside of Jesus' intervention, Shame is a never-
ending cycle.

Shame ☞

Shameful acts ☞

Even more shame

———— ·⌣ ⌣· ————

GOLDEN STEPPING STONE
Unresolved shame
is the breeding ground for perversion.

———— ·⌣ ⌣· ————

Toxic Shame

A number of years ago, all four of my wisdom
teeth were extracted. The morning of the
scheduled surgery, I woke up achy, feverish, with a slight
sore throat. Having just returned from a six-week tour
crisscrossing the country, I attributed these symptoms to
exhaustion, over-exertion of my vocal chords, and the
apprehension of the oral surgery. Absentmindedly, I neg-
lected to inform the surgeon of my symptoms. Everything
seemed to go well with the extraction, and in a few hours
I was discharged to a friend's care.

By 3:00 the next morning, my temperature was 106
degrees and I was overwhelmed with pain...hallucinat-
ing...the whole nine yards. Diagnosis? Strep and staph—
which had started in my throat—now poisoned my blood

stream. I was sick as a dog and out of commission for the next six weeks. Every few months, the infection recurred.

My doctor explained, "You have toxic infection in your blood stream. It lies dormant for a while, but given your lifestyle and schedule, you are perpetually weakened and vulnerable to recurrence of strep and staph. You will always have this toxic infection, Reba..."

I had to learn to take better care of myself and apply God's Word to my body. Occasionally, I still battle with toxic infection.

In writing this chapter, I keep thinking about "toxic shame." When we are in a weakened condition and haven't properly taken care of ourselves physically, emotionally, spiritually...we are especially vulnerable targets for recurring bouts with shame.

One of the main tenets of any 12-step substance abuse program is the acronym H.A.L.T. Beware of becoming overly

Hungry...

Angry...

Lonely...

Tired...

Twelve-step counselors teach you to deal with these issues of hunger, anger, loneliness and tiredness before they deal with you. This is good advice—not for addicts only—but for anyone.

I want to take my liberty and add another letter to the above acronym..."S"...for Sick or Shame-filled.

We can't always prevent the symptoms of sickness or shame, but we can develop a game plan for how we will combat them.

The Way Out

The cycle of toxic shame can be broken. Everyone has been caught in the shame trap at some point in our lives.

You may be wondering, "What can I do? Is there any hope for me?"

When I asked the same questions, the Lord took me by the hand and began walking me step-by-step out of the valley of shame.

Here are some of the steps I took:

Acknowledge your helplessness. I love to spend time in bookstores. The "self-help" section always amuses me—as if we can truly help ourselves...all by ourselves.

Self-help is no help at all. Self-sacrifice is the way, My way, to finding yourself, your true self. What kind of deal is it to get everything you want but lose yourself? (Matthew 16:25 TM)

The Apostle Paul affirmed, "I can do all things *through Christ* who strengthens me" (Phil. 4:13 NKJV). "*Through Christ*" is the decisive phrase. King David made it clear. "My help comes *from the Lord*" (Ps. 121:2 NKJV).

Pride and Deception conspire to convince you that you can heal yourself. But you can't deal with Baal/shame on your own. You must have the Savior's mediation.

Unmask your enemy. Recognize the source of shame is a demonic spirit trying to replace the Lord Jesus Christ as your master, lord, possessor, and husband. Expose his diabolical plot to control and destroy your life.

Dethrone him. Regardless of how shame came and established a throne in your heart, you can reclaim legal authority and occupancy from which he has ruled and dictated your life. *You need to get mad.* Not at God—not at people—but at your real enemy. When I began to see how Baal/shame was using my secrets to rob me of the ability to be fruitful, righteous indignation arose in me. I was determined to completely allow Jesus—not Baal/shame—to be my Master, Lord, Possessor, and Husband.

Through a series of events I will elaborate on in Chapter 18, the One True God of fertility blessed my barren womb...not just once, but twice! (Yes, I really am the birth mother of Destiny and Israel.)

Confess up. Or in hillbilly-eze, 'fess up. Confession is good for the soul. Look at this potent passage from James 5:16:

> *Confess to one another therefore your faults (your slips, your false steps, your offenses, your sins) and pray [also] for one another, that you may be healed and restored [to a spiritual tone of mind and heart]. The earnest (heartfelt, continued) prayer of a righteous man makes tremendous power available [dynamic in its working].*

There is great benefit in confessing our sins, problems, failings, and weaknesses, but many people are hesitant to bare their souls because they have been burned, betrayed, abused or misunderstood in the past.

My question is: "Who are you confessing to?"

James 5:14-20 demonstrates the vital role spiritual elders play in our healing, restoration, and forgiveness from sins. But many of us "confess down." By this I mean that we confess to people who are no more—or sometimes less—spiritually mature than we are.

75

The key to *"confessing to one another"* is learning to "confess up."

Let me explain: God is a God of structure and order. He places spiritually mature people over us who cover, counsel, and restore us back to wholeness.

True spiritual authority says, "How can I serve you?" not "How can I lord over you?" It speaks the truth in love and helps us grow up in every way (see Eph. 4:15). It covers a multitude of sins (see Jas. 5:20).

Look at it this way: *God has an army.*

If a sergeant has a problem, a private usually can't fix it. The sergeant needs an officer of higher rank to provide the needed strategy, covering, experience, and answers.

Ask the Lord to place you in a godly relationship with a pastor...a trustworthy, capable, anointed mentor or spiritual parent who can objectively hear your confession.

Seek a compassionate, righteous mentor who prays effectual, earnest prayers that get results...who keeps confidences...who bears good fruit in his or her own life...who can bring you back to right standing with the Lord. (See 1 Thessalonians 5:12-13.)

Our friend Dr. Mike Murdock affirms, "A mentor is not your cheerleader—but your coach. A mentor wants your success—not your comfort. A mentor is the person whose counsel you actually follow. A mentor sees something you don't see and knows something you don't know. Your mentor will always see your enemy before you do. A protégé is not the one who *needs* you—but the one who *heeds* you. Who believes something inside you will help them become all they are supposed to be."[7]

Forgive. Mark 11:25-26 evidences the most pungent reasons for extending forgiveness:

> *If you have anything against anyone, forgive him and let it drop (leave it, let it go), in order that your*

Father Who is in heaven may also forgive you your [own] failings and shortcomings and let them drop. But if you do not forgive, neither will your Father in heaven forgive your failings and shortcomings.

It's obvious, isn't it? If you want forgiveness, you must first forgive. *"Let it drop, leave it and let it go."*

Forgive your abusers.

Forgive yourself.

Forgive God.

I just heard somebody gasp for air, "Whoa, Reba! What do you mean 'forgive God'?"

It's not that God has done anything wrong. But if you are holding something against Him—or anyone—you must forgive.

Because unforgiveness is such a big issue, I don't want to deal lightly or simply "put a Band-Aid" over it. In Chapter 16, we will explore the secrets of God which empower us to finally "lay the ax to the root" of unforgiveness (see Mt. 3:10).

The bottom line. Romans 15:3 supplies the most compelling exit out of your shame:

For Christ did not please Himself [gave no thought to His own interests]; but, as it is written, The reproaches and abuses of those who reproached and abused you fell on Me...

Can you see this unparalleled benefit of salvation? Because God loves you so much, He already had a plan in place to take care of every abuse you would suffer...*before your abuse ever occurred.* Before the foundations of the earth were laid—before you were born—before anyone abused you—Jesus Christ had already taken every reproach and abuse.

Revelation 13:8 demonstrates the remedy God provided for sin, reproach and abuse...the blood of His dear Son:

...the Lamb that was slain [in sacrifice] from the foundation of the world (Revelation 13:8b).

But [you were purchased] with the precious blood of Christ (the Messiah), like that of a [sacrificial] lamb without blemish or spot. It is true that He was chosen and foreordained (destined and foreknown for it) before the foundation of the world... (1 Peter 1:19-20a).

Your reproaches and abuses fell on Jesus! By faith, release them to Him now. Cast them on the Lord.

Pile your troubles on God's shoulders—He'll carry your load, He'll help you out (Psalm 55:22 TM).

Let Him have all your worries and cares, for He is always thinking about you and watching everything that concerns you. Be careful—watch out for attacks from satan, your great enemy. He prowls around like a hungry, roaring lion, looking for some victim to tear apart. Stand firm when he attacks (1 Peter 5:7-9a TLB).

Casting your cares, anxieties, reproaches, shame and abuses on the Lord is more than a passive act of resignation. It becomes a weapon turned against the enemy.

Instead of being ashamed, My people will receive twice as much wealth. Instead of being disgraced,

Chapter 8

HALF A WOMAN
ATTRACTS HALF A MAN

What is it about the nature of the beast?

Isn't it amazing how half a woman attracts half a man?

When a man and woman enter into a covenant of marriage—even if that marriage lasts only 47 minutes—in God's eyes, they are "one flesh" (see Gen. 2:24). The mystery of marriage, of supernatural fusion into oneness, was His Genesis plan.

God regarded Adam and Eve as one entity...to the extent that when He called, "Adam,"...both would respond.

In God's divine mathematics for marriage, 1 + 1=1.

Anytime you divorce, there is a ripping apart...a tearing in two...that leaves each of you half a person. I can certainly speak from firsthand experience. Not only had I suffered this hellacious rending and subsequent shattered identity, Dony had gone through an ugly divorce too.

Trust me: *divorced ½ + divorced ½ will only equal one monstrous mess.*

Because the severing of divorce is so emotionally and spiritually traumatizing, the process back to wholeness always takes a long time. Only God can truly heal and restore you to wholeness.

When Dony and I got together, we could have been the poster children of divorce. We were vulnerable, broken, and attracted to each other like magnets.

As Grandma Luttrell clucked, "You jes' jumped from the skillet to the fryin' pan."

A Good Divorce? You Gotta Be Kidding!

*D*ivorced parties should agree to interact with civility, especially for the sake of their children; however, I never cease to be dumbfounded when someone tells me they've had "a good divorce." That's an oxymoron. There is no such thing as "a good divorce" if you comprehend the divine dynamics of the spirit realm and "one flesh."

Before I spoke at a ladies' meeting, a very attractive woman bounced across the church lobby and bubbled to her friends, "Oh, my divorce is final and I feel great!"

My ears perked up as she gushed enthusiastically, "My ex and I are still such good friends! We call each other all the time and compare notes about our new love interests..."

I wanted to shake her by the shoulders and shout, "Are you mental?!? How dumb can you get and still breathe?"

Then as I looked deeper with Spirit-eyes, I saw her with half a face...half a body...and blood spurting from every opening. The image was so real I almost gasped with horror.

Another picture immediately flashed before me: half a man's face and body loosely stitched to hers with grotesque, Frankenstein sutures. Together, they created a freaky, ghoulish monster.

Diabolical Dangers

*F*or six thousand years, satan has interacted with mankind. Millennium after millennium of toying with different strategies, temptations, accusations, and lies has made him an expert on human behavior. He's a master manipulator who knows every vulnerable "hot button" to push. His methods and patterns are consistent and definable.

Wrong Relationships

*W*hen your soul is ripped in two by divorce, very often you are seized with panic to fill the void of separation.

Misery really does love company. Half a woman attracts half a man...and vice versa.

Like spirits are drawn to one another.

Pain attracts pain.

Hurt attracts hurt.

Rejection attracts rejection.

I've seen it happen time and time again.

Unless you grasp the truth that your healing and wholeness are found in Father's arms, in Father's house, in Father's ways—the enemy can use this highly charged, vulnerable period of life to set you up for more failure. The deceiver will plant a wrong relationship appearing to contain all the ingredients you need. This person will seem to possess whatever is lacking in you or your previous relationship.

For example, if your husband left you for another woman, you may feel as though you lack beauty, charm, sex appeal, intelligence, social graces, or some other attribute.

83

Along comes Mr. Wrong who tells you what a fool your husband was to leave such a wonderful woman like you.

"You're beautiful, sexy, intelligent, desirable..."

What happens?

Vulnerable *you* falls for it hook, line, and sinker. While you may actually possess these qualities, that's really not the point. Of necessity, you must surrender to the lengthy process of being made whole again before venturing into the shark-infested waters of new romantic relationships.

When you've been ripped apart by divorce—half a person—your identity has been jeopardized.

No human relationship, not even a good one, can take the Lord's place in restoring you to wholeness.

Too Busy to Be

God created you to be whole and complete—spirit, soul, and body.

Psalm 23 is one of the most familiar passages in the entire Bible. In fact, it is so familiar that it is easy to skim over the simple, profound, life-changing truth: *God wants to restore your soul.* Your soul is your will, mind, thoughts, emotions, appetites, desires, and self.

Slowly read this timeless passage.

Absorb the Truth.

Let it sink in.

The Lord is my Shepherd [to feed, guide, and shield me]. I shall not lack. He makes me lie down in [fresh, tender] green pastures; He leads me beside the still and restful waters. **[He restores my soul.]** *He refreshes and restores my life (my self); He leads me in the paths of righteousness [uprightness and right standing with Him—not for my earning it, but] for His name's sake* (Psalm 23:1-3).

84

The restoration of your soul is a private, personal experience between God and you. Soul restoration comes about in an atmosphere of quiet, still waters and will rest and refresh your entire self.

Beware. The enemy of self will try anything and everything to keep you from becoming still, tranquil, calm, and quiet.

In today's society, we are inundated with noise, clatter, and distractions. We have become overwhelmed with commotion and activity...and are increasingly nervous and uneasy with peace and quiet.

How long does it takes you to unwind when you go on vacation? Even then, many vacations are run here, run there—see this, see that. We need a vacation after we come home from vacation.

If you want to see some people become really uncomfortable, just get into a church service where the Spirit of the Lord takes complete control and no one sings, preaches, prays, plays music, or does anything but wait in silence.

We are conditioned for *doing* instead of *being*.

I think we often fail to remember God created human beings—not human doings.

We must break our detrimental habits of busy-ness and noisy-ness...and let the Good Shepherd lead us beside still waters of refreshing and restoration. There...He rebuilds, reconstructs, recreates, and restores my soul!

———— ·⌣ ⌣· ————

GOLDEN STEPPING STONE
To BE or not to BE.
That is the question.

———— ·⌣ ⌣· ————

85

Every divorce is unique and different, but I believe the following counsel works for anyone who has experienced or is now going through divorce.

Get Single Again

*W*hile you are repairing and mending is *not* the time to date someone new. Rushing into new relationships may actually deter the healing process.

Why are you in such a hurry to get back into the dating game?

Are you afraid to be alone?

Afraid to be single?

There's a major difference between being alone and being lonely.

Do yourself a favor.

Take a time out!

I recommend healing at least one year after divorce before getting involved romantically again.[1] Or why not approach it a whole new way? Wait on God to bring you into the right relationship instead of taste-testing from the dating buffet.

The only way to get single again is to let Holy Spirit sever the soul ties.

Let Him "un-crowd" your bed.

For example—if you dated a lot of different people and gave parts of your heart to each one, when you eventually do marry—you are asking your spouse to sleep in a "crowded bed." Then if you go through the hell of divorce and quickly remarry without having healed, you are asking your next spouse to sleep in an even more crowded bed. Unfortunately, if you are one who jumps from one relationship to another, you may wake up one morning and realize the only thing that's changed is the color of your lover's eyes.

———— •ɔ ↭• ————

GOLDEN STEPPING STONE
Let the Lord
"un-crowd" your bed.

———— •ɔ ↭• ————

Take Time for Yourself

*G*et to know yourself. Rediscover *the real you* that's probably buried deep beneath the rubble of a cataclysmic divorce or broken relationship.

If you are divorced, you probably don't know what it means to be kind to yourself.

To love yourself.

To like yourself.

Is there something you would like to do for *you?*

Go back to school? Get in shape? Travel? Attend seminars? Revive a long lost hobby? Learn to play a musical instrument? Have quality time with your children? Write that novel? Pursue a new career?

Let Jesus "Husband" You

*D*on't be afraid to wait on the Lord. Get to know Him. Really *know* Him. Nothing will heal you like bonding and intimacy with Him.

I count everything as loss compared to the possession of the priceless privilege (the overwhelming preciousness, the surpassing worth, and supreme advantage) of knowing Christ Jesus my Lord and of progressively becoming more deeply and intimately acquainted with Him [of perceiving and recognizing and understanding Him more fully and clearly] (Philippians 3:8a).

Male or female—you can marry yourself to Christ, the Anointed One, and His anointing. Since you are the Bride of Christ, let Him "husband" you. Become one with Him.

Don't Isolate Yourself

*O*pen yourself to "Jesus with skin on"—the people He will use to reach and touch you...your children, extended family, friends, mentors, professional and spiritual counselors. Let Him use them to put you up in His feather bed...feed you the chicken soup of His Word...cradle you in His rocking chair...and nurse you to wholeness.

The Web

*G*od uses safe people in safe houses, but the black-widowed enemy wants to seduce hapless victims into his dangerous parlor.

Glen and Sharon were best friends with Mitch and Wendy. Glen and Mitch compared business investments while Sharon and Wendy spent hours chatting on the phone every week. When Wendy unexpectedly left Mitch for a man at her job and refused contact with family and friends, everyone was devastated.

Mitch lost his wife.

Sharon lost her best friend.

Glen lost a good bridge partner.

Glen wanted to reach out and comfort poor Mitch, but words didn't come easily for him. Besides, business was booming and he had little time for anything else. Glen encouraged his wife, who was a natural caregiver, to spend some time with lonely, grieving Mitch. But Glen didn't detect that Sharon was also lonely and grieving.

In reality, Glen's lack of communication skills coupled with workaholic tendencies had contributed to the deep void in Sharon.

How many of her lovingly prepared, candlelit dinners had gone uneaten?

How many nights had she patiently waited in a sexy negligee only to have Glen come home and fall into bed too exhausted or disinterested?

Mitch, on the other hand, was an emotional wreck—half a man—who really needed to talk. He hated eating meals alone. He craved a hand to hold. He was desperate for the companionship and attention of someone like Sharon. Sharon was fractured and unfulfilled—half a woman—who was equally needy.

Soon their casual conversations shifted from Wendy and the divorce to heart-to-heart intimacies. Before they knew it, they had fallen into the trap of two "half" people believing they could find happiness and completion in each other's arms.

What began as harmless *compassion* turned into unbridled *passion*.

Important Key

*H*ow could they have avoided this trap?

There are many answers to this complicated question, but I want to deal with one specifically.

Sharon needed to learn that no matter how much compassion she felt for Mitch, she was setting them both up for disaster when she agreed to spend time alone with any man other than her own husband.

One of my spiritual fathers, Bishop Earl Paulk, whom God used to rescue Dony and me when our marriage was on the rocks, taught us a life-changing spiritual principle: *never minister mercy alone, especially with someone of the opposite sex.*

Adhering to this vital principle keeps the doors of seduction and deception closed. It protects both parties. You may feel absolutely no attraction yourself—but the other person can easily misconstrue your compassion and enter into a fantasy or false relationship.

The definition of *fantasy* is "the process of creating unrealistic or improbable mental images in response to a psychological need."[2]

Colossians 3:5 (KJV) refers to fantasies as "inordinate affections."

Even when extending compassion and mercy to members of the same sex, it is wise to have a third party involved for clarity and protection.

GOLDEN STEPPING STONE
*Never minister mercy alone,
especially with someone of the opposite sex.*

Unfortunately, the Sharon and Mitch scenario plays on too many stages and wrecks too many homes. Pride makes you believe it can never happen to you. As my wise ole grandmother admonished, "An ounce of prevention is worth a pound of cure."

Grandma was right.

Leave no [such] room or foothold for the devil [give no opportunity to him] (Ephesians 4:27).

90

Do not therefore let what seems good to you be con-sidered an evil thing [by someone else] (Romans 14:16).

Isolation

*F*or someone going through the battlefield of divorce and emerging from the trenches as half a person—the pain, guilt and shame are overwhelming. As a Christian, you often carry extra burdens—condemnation and religious guilt—because not only have you disappointed yourself and others, you may feel as though you have failed God as well.

Here you are: You've stepped onto an emotional land-mine. You're wounded, maimed, broken, and bleeding.

Walking around with a concussion of the soul.

How can you even think right?

You desperately need to get to God's hospital for emer-gency treatment, but the adversary will try anything to keep you away from that life-giving flow of oil and wine. He will try to convince you to retreat from the Body of Christ be-cause he knows that is where your healing will begin.

Satan understands this basic principle: If your finger is cut off, it will live for a while. But if it isn't reattached to the body and the blood flow started again, it will soon die.

The life of the flesh is in the blood (Leviticus 17:11a KJV).

Let's make it plain: Your enemy does not want you to be healed. He wants to keep you out of God's house and isolate you from God's people. Only spiritual people can truly restore you.

Brethren, if any person is overtaken in misconduct or sin of any sort, you who are spiritual [who are

91

responsive to and controlled by the Spirit] should set him right and restore and reinstate him, without any sense of superiority and with all gentleness.... Bear (endure, carry) one another's burdens and troublesome moral faults, and in this way fulfill and observe perfectly the law of Christ (the Messiah) and complete what is lacking... (Galatians 6:1-2).

After citing this great passage of Scripture, I can picture someone scowl, "Reba, is all divorce sin?"

Let's face it: Divorce is a "hot button"...a very complicated, controversial issue affecting more than one in two marriages in North America. Most everyone has strongly held convictions on the subject. But one definition of *sin* is "missing the mark."[3]

Regardless of whose fault the divorce is—somebody missed the mark.

Somebody sinned.

Even if you are a victim of divorce—you still end up half a person who must be healed and restored.

Another Trap

*T*he enemy works in subtle ways: if you do go to church, you will probably arrive late...sit in the back row...and leave early to avoid personal contact with fellow believers.

Satan fully understands there is a proximity to the anointing. He wants you to keep your distance.[4]

As you are drawn away, the Lord's still, small Voice becomes very difficult to distinguish above the sinister cacophony.

Shame sneers, "You are such a bad person. Such a failure. No one in the Church will even want to be around you."

92

Disgrace insinuates, "You will be treated differently now that you're plagued with the leprosy of divorce."

Fear gibes, "What makes you think God could still love you? If He can't—His children sure won't."

Deceit woos, "Why don't you just pull away from everyone? Fast. Pray. Get alone with God."

Seduction purrs, "The Church is full of hypocrites. Why don't you just go party with your old unsaved friends?"

How do you silence the roar of these confusing, intimidating voices? You begin by returning to Jesus Christ, the Source of life, help, strength, sanity, peace, love, joy, and restoration. He is the only "Way, Truth and Life" (see Jn. 14:6).

Jesse Duplantis says it this way to believers: "Since Jesus is the Way, you can never truly be lost. Since Jesus is the Truth, you can never truly be deceived. Since Jesus is the Life, the devil can't kill you."

The bottom line: Keep your heart open to hear the Voice. Pour your heart out to Him in prayer. Read the Word daily. Allow yourself to be embraced by loving medics in God's hospital who are trained and skilled at saving lives.

Don't despise the process.

You may not see it now, but the Lord *is* making something beautiful out of the mess of your life.

He has made everything beautiful in its time (Ecclesiastes 3:11a NIV).

————— • ⌣ ⌣ • —————

GOLDEN STEPPING STONE
Anytime you're hurting,
run to the Doctor! Run to His hospital!

————— • ⌣ ⌣ • —————

Take courage from this promise-filled passage of Scripture:

> *The Spirit of the Lord God is upon Me, because the Lord has anointed Me to preach good tidings to the poor; He has sent Me to heal the brokenhearted, to proclaim liberty to the captives, and the opening of the prison to those who are bound; to proclaim the acceptable year of the Lord, and the day of vengeance of our God; to comfort all who mourn, to console those who mourn in Zion, to give them beauty for ashes, the oil of joy for mourning, the garment of praise for the spirit of heaviness; that they may be called trees of righteousness, the planting of the Lord, that He may be glorified.... Instead of your shame you shall have double honor, and instead of confusion they shall rejoice in their portion. Therefore in their land they shall possess double; everlasting joy shall be theirs* (Isaiah 61:1-3,7 NKJV).

Endnotes

1. I highly recommend *I Kissed Dating Good-bye* by Joshua Harris (Sisters, OR: Multnomah Publishers Inc., 1997). This book has become mandatory reading for the young people who intern with our ministry. (If you have a teenager, read it together.) Another excellent book on the subject of singleness and celibacy is *No More Sheets* by Juanita Bynum (Lanham, MD: Pneuma Life Publishing, 1998).

2. *Webster's Medical Desk Dictionary* (Springfield, MA: Merriam-Webster, 1996), p. 235. Used by permission.

3. *Strong's Exhaustive Concordance* (Iowa Falls, IA: World Bible Publishers, Inc., 1989), G264.

4. Isaiah 14:12-17 and Ezekiel 28:12-18 describe Lucifer's proximity to God's anointing. He was the covering cherub nearest to God Almighty. Through pride, he was cast down from Heaven, taking one-third of the angelic hosts with him. He still tries to put distance between God and man.

"Don't Give Up"

Don't give up!
When your heart is bruised and broken
Disappointed by your friends
You're feeling all alone
Don't give up!
Through the bitter tears keep trying
He'll pick you up, bind your wounds
mend your heart
'Cause we have a Promise—a Person to cling to
He won't let us go through more than we can bear

Don't give up!
If you don't understand His way of teaching
He's working everything together for good
Don't give up!
Even when the world says you are defeated
Just thank our God who causes us to triumph in the Lord
Don't give up!

Don't give up!
Though the howling storm is raging
He makes the clouds His chariots
He rides upon the wind
Don't give up!
Though you fear you'll drown in sorrow
With eyes of faith look up to Him and be saved
'Cause we have a Promise—a Person to cling to
He won't let us go through more than we can bear
Don't give up! [e]

Chapter 9

"LORD, CHANGE ME"

What is it about 3:00 in the morning?

*D*oes God talk louder or do I just listen better? It had been one hell of a night. Dony had come home early from the recording studio in another drunken, jealous rage. But then again...it was Tuesday...and Tuesday's storms were as predictable as *"red sky at morning, sailors take warning."*

I had been accepted into an exclusive acting class under the tutelage of one of Hollywood's premier drama coaches. I eagerly anticipated the three-hour Tuesday afternoon sessions, which awakened my dormant acting abilities, nurtured my hungry creativity, and stretched my self-imposed artistic limitations. Directors and casting agents for films, television, and Broadway productions often observed our classes through a one-way glass, and had voiced special interest in me. Both my coach and agent were convinced of my potential for a lucrative acting career and were frustrated with me for not going on more

97

auditions or accepting major roles. But they didn't understand my reasons for taking the class.

This was something I did for *me*.

It was much less about artistic success and much more about escape from the torturous reality my life with Dony had become.

As much as I absolutely loved my acting class—Dony absolutely hated it. For those three hours, I was free from his stifling control. Just getting away from the dark clouds of confusion and chaos gave me a clearer perspective.

I decided to take advantage of the drive time each week to begin opening my heart to the Lord. I recognized Dony's insatiable addiction was making me almost as crazy as he was. Every day I lied and covered for him. But in the solitude of my car, I poured out my desperation and tried to tune my spirit to the Voice.

How I treasured those precious few hours!

For those three hours plus drive time—heaven forbid if I ever got stuck in traffic—Dony's addicted mind speculated wildly about my supposed affairs with acting partners, coaches, and anyone else I might have contact with between class and home.

How he resented those precious few hours!

One Tuesday afternoon, my whole body tensed as I heard tires screech to a halt in the driveway, keys fumble in the lock, a shoulder ram against the unyielding door, incessant ringing of the bell, and familiar slurred curses. For the sake of maintaining respectability with our neighbors, Dony usually saved the violence for inside the house. But today he was reckless, irrational, and over the edge.

Long, curly black hair fell in sweaty tendrils across his scowling forehead. Reeking from a nauseating concoction of vodka, marijuana, after-shave and Hall's cough drops, he stumbled into the foyer, slammed the door, and bellowed, "Reba! Where are you?"

I would pay dearly this Tuesday.

The next hours of tormenting mind games, relentless accusations, cruel innuendo, and crazed threats ended with Dony trashing my freshly scrubbed kitchen.

Something new and more horrifying was smoldering in his eyes. Something greater than his abiding fear of my 6'3" father. This Tuesday, the demons weren't satisfied with merely smashing another set of dishes.

They wanted to smash me.

Self-preservation kicked in. I rushed down the corridor to Dony's office, picked up a phone, and forced my mind to try and remember somebody's phone number.

Anybody's!

Who should I call? My parents? The police?

Dony was hot on my heels. He jerked the receiver out of my hand, slammed it onto the cradle, and spun me around.

"Think you're gonna call your mommy and daddy?" he taunted maniacally, his face perilously close to mine. "Nobody's gonna save you this time!"

I was instantly furious. He had unearthed a dormant core of red-hot outrage smoldering deep inside me. How dare he threaten me! I intentionally provoked him with a renewed surge of anger.

"You wanna hurt me, Dony McGuire? Go ahead and try!!"

Incensed by the unexpected comeback, he shoved me so hard into the black leather chair that my teeth rattled.

"Okay," he railed. "Just don't forget...*you* asked for it!"

The muscles in his arm tightened as he drew back his open hand, his fingers taut, white, and menacing. Instinctively I braced myself, aware he was actually going to

99

strike me. In slow motion, his powerful jab targeted my face. I squinched my eyes and was shocked when his aim veered at the last second and struck my upraised hands instead.

With each whack, he shrieked obscenities.

"You slut!"

Slap.

"Whore!"

Slap.

"Bitch!"

Slap.

Each smack increased in intensity. My fingertips shuddered, wrists threatened to snap, forearms vibrated into the sockets of my shoulders. Daggers of fire stabbed my bones, muscles, joints, and ligaments, exploding into pinpoint infernos and broken veins.

I won't give him the satisfaction of screaming, I resolved internally, shrinking from hideous reality into my child-hood abyss of numbness. Nothing could touch me there.

·⁔ ⌣·

*D*ony momentarily boomeranged to a sobered mind, recognizing he had plunged to new depths of alcoholic rage. This couldn't be happening! He had never laid a hand on any woman. This time he knew he had gone too far.

Squeezing his head so hard his skull almost cracked, he sobbed, "Oh my God! What have I done? What have I done? ..."

He sank slowly to the floor and succumbed to the perilous undertow of drugged blackness.

·⁔ ⌣·

*D*runks aren't the only ones who have blackouts.

My next memory was finding Dony passed out on the floor under his desk. I don't know why I even cared...I guess the perpetual caregiver side of my personality was invariably compelled to drag my comatose husband from his office to our bedroom at the other end of the house. He was all dead weight.

To be honest, if I had to do it over again, I would have left the fool lying on the floor!

Hoisting him onto the poster bed, I noticed a Bible lying on my nightstand.

"That's it!" I cried with a sudden burst of inspiration. "I'm gonna get the Word of God into you...one way or another!"

I gleefully scoured the house for every single translation of the Bible I could find. Arms piled high, I carried them back to the bedroom, opened them up and strategically placed them one by one over Dony's sprawled body.

"Is that all of 'em? Wonder if I missed any?" I mused, absentmindedly swiping my runny nose on the back of my aching hand, making a quick mental note to buy more *Kleenex*.

With a stroke of genius, I suddenly remembered the closet doorstop: one of those old-time-holy-lookin'-cream-colored-leatherbound-gilded-page-gigantic-thirty-two-pound family Bibles I had picked up at a yard sale for $4.99. (It was great for pressing flowers and in a pinch could also be used as a stepstool.) Now I contemplated an even better idea..."a good thing from Martha Stewart."

"I oughta lay this sucker open right across your face, Dony McGuire...and press ever so gently," I cackled with psycho, Norman Bates glee. "I could probably even get away with it!"

I envisioned next week's tabloid headlines: *GRAMMY WINNER DIES MYSTERIOUSLY IN BED–SUFFOCATED BY SCRIPTURES?...FINISHED OFF BY FAMILY BIBLE?...KILLED BY KING JAMES?...ASPHIXIATED BY AUTHORIZED VERSION?...WALLOPED BY THE WORD?*

My, the possibilities were endless!

For just a brief moment, I could see the humor in the insanity. Then the sobering realization hit me: *I really was capable of murder.*

Falling to my knees, I pulled the big old Bible to my chest and sobbed, "Father, You've gotta help me. Please..."

Some times desperation is a wonderful thing. It pushes you to ask the right questions. It forges a key to unlock just the right doors.

"Lord, teach me how to pray for my husband."

I had prayed countless prayers for Dony's deliverance, but never had I asked God to show me how. I was humbled by the irony. *I* who knew so little had been talking to One who knows everything, and *I* had been doing all the talking! Now I was prepared to listen and learn.

Hearing the Lord's audible Voice startled me. *"Pray this, Reebs...pray 'Lord...'"* He paused, waiting for my response, so I did.

"Lord..."

"Change..."

"Change..."

"Me."

"Wait a minute! You see that man up there in that bed full of Bibles?" I protested. *"He's* the problem."

I figured God must not know so I proceeded to tell Him in vivid detail all about Dony's addictions, sins, failings...I think I even threw in a parking violation or two. The amazing thing about God was that He allowed me to rant and rave without once interrupting. When I felt I had finally set the record straight, I said, "Now...teach me how to pray for my husband."

Pray this, Reebs. Pray 'Lord...'

Lord...

Change...

Change...

Me.

Me?

I want you to lift up Jesus...so the Christ in you will draw Dony to Himself.

That was *not* what I wanted to hear!

It got worse.

I want you to serve Dony as if he was Christ.

Yuk! Gag me with a maggot! You've gotta be kidding!

I want you to call the things that are not as though they were...and see a potential Christ in Dony.

A potential Christ?

I looked over at my husband lying spread-eagled on the bed. One thing was in my favor: Dony had a "Jesus look" happening. Long, dark hair. Beard. Piercing eyes. (Thank God, he wasn't bald or toothless and didn't weigh five hundred pounds!)

Once again, desperation asked the right question.

Can You help me, Father?

Would you like Me to send you the Helper?

I wasn't quite sure what He meant, but it sounded right. A blanket of peace settled over me and I fell asleep with my head on my King James murder-weapon-turned-pillow-of-promises.

A Picture Is Worth a Thousand Words

Sounds like a sick soap opera, doesn't it? But this wasn't some TV show scripted by over-imaginative Hollywood writers.

This was our life.

A certified mess.

Unfortunately, real life afternoon dramas like ours are played out in households all over the world. That's the sad truth.

With every lesson the Lord was teaching me, He painted a picture to help me visualize it. He used everyday objects to trigger my memory of these simple, life-changing truths.

A couple of days after my "Lord, change me" experience, I was emptying out a favorite purse and retrieved a handful of loose coins from the bottom.

I am pleased you have prayed 'Lord, change me'...but this can't be a one-time prayer.

What do you mean?

You must continually maintain an attitude of change-ability. Look in your hand, Reebs. What do you see?

Uh...a handful of change?

Exactly. Let that change ever remind you that I AM changing you a little at a time. The more willing you are to be changed...to be flexible and moldable in My hand...the quicker the process.

To this day, any time I'm shopping and a store clerk drops shiny coins into my hand—those quarters, dimes, nickels or pennies become faithful reminders. I smile and remember to pray, "Lord, change me."

Bear in mind: change is a perpetual process.

The goal?

To be changed into His image. To look like Jesus.

...[your] new [spiritual self] which is [ever in the process of being] renewed and remolded into [fuller and more perfect knowledge upon] knowledge after

the image (the likeness) of Him Who created it (Colossians 3:10).

———— •◡ ◡• ————

GOLDEN STEPPING STONE
Be courageous enough to pray
"Lord, change me."

———— •◡ ◡• ————

Reba's Belly Buttons?

I'd like to interject a few personal feelings and observations about abusive relationships. My opinion, if you please.

(An opinion is kind of like a belly button. Everybody since Adam has got one. Or as my friend Dr. Rodney Howard-Browne contends, "Opinions are like armpits. Everybody has at least two of them...and sometimes they stink!")

You gotta have emotional closure. The closure I'm talking about is not based on someone else; it's *you* dealing with the issues inside you.

Unfinished emotional business is like walking around with a festering, open wound. As my mother would say, "You're in a bad way, baby."

Are you B.A.D.? Bitter...Angry...Depressed.

If you realize that you are still B.A.D., you don't have emotional closure.

Unless you allow the Lord to really change you, you will carry "baggage"—beastly bitterness, agonizing anger, debilitating depression, wounded ways, toxic tendencies, paralyzing patterns—into your next marriage or relationship.

A good flight instructor warns fledgling pilots, "Never make decisions when you're upside down. Get turned around, get your nose up and get your wings straight... then re-chart your course."

Your abuser is not your enemy. We waste precious time and energy warring against a person rather than the demonic spirits influencing or oppressing the person. This is not just my opinion—it's the Word.

> *For we are not fighting against people made of flesh and blood, but against persons without bodies—the evil rulers of the unseen world, those mighty satanic beings and great evil princes of darkness who rule this world; and against huge numbers of wicked spirits in the spirit world* (Ephesians 6:12 TLB).

Oftentimes, we mistakenly fight against someone with a human face rather than "a huge number of wicked spirits...people without bodies."

We're wrestling the wrong opponent. We have met the enemy—and it sure ain't us. Our anger is misfocused and misrouted. And to make matters worse, we feel ashamed for feeling angry because most people are taught it is a sin to get angry. So we either lash out or internalize the fact we're outraged, furious, or spittin' mad.

Let me make it clear: There is a place for anger. You can be angry without careening over the edge into sin.

> *Go ahead and be angry. You do well to be angry—but don't use your anger as fuel for revenge. And don't stay angry. Don't go to bed angry. Don't give the devil that kind of foothold in your life* (Ephesians 4:26-27 TM).

I can hear someone say, "Jesus had a temper. He sure let 'em have it when He threw the moneychangers out of the Temple!"

There's a world of difference between temper and righteous anger.

When Jesus cast the moneychangers from the Temple, you better believe He was angry because a wicked priesthood had corrupted the holy act of worship by selling blemished sacrifices for exorbitant prices and unblemished animals at outrageous prices. Many worshipers traveled great distances to offer sacrifice at the Jerusalem Temple and had no easy way to transport a perfect sacrifice. Consequently, they were forced to purchase animals at the Temple from perverted, greedy priests who often charged ten times the fair market value for animals suitable for offering to the Lord.

Jesus was justifiably angry and drove out those wicked, unscrupulous men. (Scholars estimate it took Him approximately two to three hours to clean them out.)

Jesus dealt with an ungodly system righteously, quickly, and efficiently.

He didn't let the sun set on His wrath.

He didn't give the devil any kind of foothold in His life.

His anger was focused on the right target.

———— ⋅◡◟⋅ ————

GOLDEN STEPPING STONE
Your abuser is not your enemy.

———— ⋅◡◟⋅ ————

When is enough...enough? Sometimes we bail out from a bad relationship before we have exhausted every possi means of resolution and rehabilitation. Check out the next verses in Ephesians 6.

> *...having done all [the crisis demands], to stand [firmly in your place]. Stand...* (Ephesians 6:13-14).

Noted psychologist Dr. Phillip C. McGraw teaches, "Sometimes you make the right decision, sometimes you have to make the decision right."[1]

I couldn't agree more.

Have you really done "all that your crisis demands"? Is there anything inside *you* that you've been unwilling to let the Lord change? Have you earned the right to call it quits?

When you're riding an emotional roller coaster is not the time to bail out or make life-changing decisions. Postpone making major choices when you're in the heat of the battle...when your thoughts are spinning in a raging tornado...when your nerves are raw and ragged...when you have closeted yourself in a dark room or sunken into deep depression.

You need to pray "Lord, change me" out of love for yourself. You need to get yourself strong enough—to be well able—to come to the right conclusions.

How can you get strong?

First, let me deal with some basics I learned from the NEWSTART® program pioneered at the world-renowned ᵂ‌ᵉⁱ...te in Weimar, California.[2] NEWSTART® is a ...remember acronym:

...rition. Are you eating nutritiously? ...u consuming plenty of fresh fruits ...getables every day? Is your diet large- ...prised of fat laden, processed foods?

If your body is nutritionally depleted, you will likely suffer chemical imbalances that affect your health, energy levels, attitudes, moods, etc. High fat junk food and caffeinated beverages are especially harmful.

- **E—exercise.** Are you exercising regularly? God didn't create our bodies to be sedentary. The vast majority of North Americans do not exercise enough. Just walking four or five miles a day even three or four times a week will cause dramatic changes in your whole being.

- **W—water.** Are you drinking eight to ten glasses of water every day? Inadequate intake of water means you are probably dehydrated. The immune system becomes weakened to fight against disease. The kidneys can't flush out the impurities from the blood stream. It's like pouring a single cup of water into a sink heaped with dirty, greasy dishes and expecting them to come out squeaky clean. It ain't gonna happen! (Remember: coffee and sodas don't count as "drinking water.")

- **S—sunlight.** Are you getting enough sunlight every day? The sun and bright light trigger a response to two important hormones, which are largely responsible for preventing the blues: the "feel good" seratonin and the "good sleep" melatonin (produced by the pineal gland in the eye). Seratonin and melatonin are stimulated when sunlight hits our eyes. That's why some people become more depressed in the winter months when days are shorter and darker. Two hours of morning sun is very effective in lifting depression.

- **T—temperance.** Are you out of control in any area of your life? One of the most overlooked "fruit of the Spirit"[3] is temperance or self-control. It is essential that we submit our thoughts, wills, emotions, appetites, and every potential out-of-control part of our beings to Holy Spirit.

- **A—air.** Are you breathing fresh, cleansing air? Inhaling deeply and fully expanding the lungs?

- **R—rest.** How much rest and sleep are you getting each night? Research reveals that we need eight or nine hours of uninterrupted sleep in order to complete the three cycles of sleep necessary to rest and rejuvenate the body. On the other hand, excessive sleeping is a sure sign of depression or some physical malady.

- **T—trust in God.** Do you make a daily practice of surrendering to the Lord? Are you trusting your whole life to God? Trust is the highest form of faith. Believing God is "working everything together for your good" (see Rom. 8:28) even when you can't see how He's doing it. Trusting Him when you can't trace Him.

NEWSTART® is basically adopting a Garden of Eden mentality.

Following these natural stepping stones will lead you to a stronger, more stable physical and emotional state of being.

It's you doing your part and letting the Lord do His.

———— •ɔ ↺• ————

GOLDEN STEPPING STONE
Let the Lord help you make a new start.

———— •ɔ ↺• ————

Should I stay or go? I believe that no woman, no child, no senior citizen—nobody—should ever stay in a physically abusive or life-threatening situation. I shouldn't have stayed, but I did...and believe me, I paid dearly.

I can hear someone ask, "Are you saying I should get a divorce?"

Don't read what I'm not writing. I am not advising or advocating anyone to divorce. That's not my place.

First of all, God hates divorce and so do I.

For the Lord, the God of Israel, says: I hate divorce and marital separation and him who covers his garment [his wife] with violence. Therefore keep a watch upon your spirit [that it may be controlled by My Spirit], that you deal not treacherously and faithlessly [with your marriage mate] (Malachi 2:16).

Secondly, while I pray you receive wisdom and strategies from this book, I am not your personal counselor. It wouldn't be fair to you or me to be cast into that role. You need a counselor who can look you eye-to-eye and walk you through the entire healing and restoration to wholeness process—a Spirit-led, tough-love advisor who has a clear perspective of the individuals and situation.

If you are being abused, I don't believe God expects you to stay and be tormented or injured.

Get to a safe house away from the danger and madness.[4] A quiet place where you can hear from God and receive ministry. The enemy will always try to convince you there is no such place...or your abuser will find you...or your leaving will only make matters worse.

Because of the complex nature of co-dependency, by this point in the relationship, most likely you have been browbeaten, demoralized, and convinced that you could never survive without the abuser...never make it on your own...never adequately provide for yourself and your children. That's the nature of the spirit of control: to manipulate you into absolute dependence on the controller. Typically, unbridled control will eventually lead to abuse and violence physically, emotionally, mentally.

Have a Plan B. If you are in a potentially life-threatening situation, start now to make a back-up plan of escape.

Pray. Get the mind of God. (Read Proverbs 16:1-4.)

Talk with your pastor or trusted counselor. Hopefully, you won't have to run for your life.

Exceeding Precious Promises

I will deal with abuse in greater detail in other chapters, but for now let me offer you some of the precious promises the Lord used to comfort and sustain me.

> *For by wise counsel you can wage your war, and in an abundance of counselors there is victory and safety* (Proverbs 24:6).

> *Have mercy on me and be gracious to me, O Lord, for I am weak (faint and withered away); O Lord,*

heal me, for my bones are troubled. My [inner] self [as well as my body] is also exceedingly disturbed and troubled. But You, O Lord, how long [until You return and speak peace to me]? Return [to my relief], O Lord, deliver my life; save me for the sake of Your steadfast love and mercy. For in death there is no remembrance of You; in Sheol (the place of the dead) who will give You thanks? I am weary with my groaning; all night I soak my pillow with tears, I drench my couch with my weeping. My eye grows dim because of grief; it grows old because of all my enemies. Depart from me, all you workers of iniquity, for the Lord has heard the voice of my weeping. The Lord has heard my supplication; the Lord receives my prayer. Let all my enemies be ashamed and sorely troubled; let them turn back and be put to shame suddenly (Psalm 6:2-10).

You are a hiding place for me; You, Lord, preserve me from trouble, You surround me with songs and shouts of deliverance... (Psalm 32:7).

In You, O Lord, do I put my trust and seek refuge; let me never be put to shame or [have my hope in You] disappointed; deliver me in Your righteousness! Bow down Your ear to me, deliver me speedily! Be my Rock of refuge, a strong Fortress to save me! Yes, You are my Rock and my Fortress; therefore for Your name's sake, lead me and guide me. Draw me out of the net that they have laid secretly for me, for You are my Strength and my Stronghold (Psalm 31:1-4).

Endnotes

1. *Life Strategies*, Dr. Phillip C. McGraw, Ph.D. (New York: Hyperion Books, 1999), p. 182.

2. NEWSTART® is the registered trademark for the Weimar Institute, a Christian wellness center near Sacramento, California. The NEWSTART® acronym is used by permission of the Weimar Institute, PO Box 486, Weimar, CA 95736. Telephone: 1-800-525-9192. I highly recommend the NEWSTART® Program to anyone struggling with medical issues or desiring better health. Their holistic approach, coupled with prayer and spiritual counseling, has helped thousands around the world.

3. Galatians 5:22-23. "The fruit of the [Holy] Spirit [the work which His presence within accomplishes] is love, joy (gladness), peace, patience (an even temper, forbearance), kindness, goodness (benevolence), faithfulness, gentleness (meekness, humility), self-control (self-restraint, continence). Against such things there is no law [that can bring a charge]."

4. Jeremiah 15:18-21. "Why is my pain perpetual and my wound incurable, refusing to be healed? Will You indeed be to me like a deceitful brook, like waters that fail and are uncertain? Therefore thus says the Lord [to Jeremiah]: If you return [and give up this mistaken tone of distrust and despair], then I will give you again a settled place of quiet and safety, and you will be My minister; and if you separate the precious from the vile [cleansing your own heart from unworthy and unwarranted suspicions concerning God's faithfulness], you shall be My mouthpiece. [But do not yield to them.] Let them return to you— not you to [the people]. And I will make you to this people a fortified, bronze wall; they will fight against you, but they will not prevail over you, for I am with you to save and deliver you, says the Lord. And I will deliver you out of the hands of the wicked, and I will redeem you out of the palms of the terrible and ruthless tyrants."

Occasionally,
you pray to see angels
or Jesus
or some heavenly vision.
But when it really happens,
what are you supposed to do?

Somehow there was a knowing deep inside...
Holy Spirit wanted to walk with me
through my everyday life.

Chapter 10

I Decide What I Wear

What is it about happy birds?

They coo and warble merrily outside a bedroom window, oblivious to the storm raging inside. Birds must not know what Wednesdays mean.

Their morning song was my alarm clock as I stirred from a crumpled heap on the thick Persian rug. Throbbing temples, stiffened joints, and puffy eyes were solemn reminders of how much I hated "the morning after."

I slowly reached for the carved Chippendale bedpost to pull myself up and winced from the excruciating pain shooting through my hands. They were discolored, swollen, and looked as though they belonged to somebody else. I flexed tender fingers, attempting unsuccessfully to ease my wedding band over enlarged, uncooperative knuckles.

There was Dony. Still sprawled out. Still covered with Bibles.

I dragged myself to the bathroom and forced a reluctant peek into the mirror. There were the familiar telltale signs of Tuesday's battles, but...

What's that on my cheek?

I dampened a wash cloth and gently rubbed the red marks on my face. I rubbed and rubbed but the weird redness wasn't going away.

What in the world? What are those marks? Are those... letters?

On closer examination, I saw that the engraved, Gothic letters 'L'...'E' from my "HOLY BIBLE pillow" were imprinted just beneath my left cheekbone.

Wonder if this is what Cain looked like when he got the mark of God after killing Abel.

I laughed quietly.

At least I didn't kill Dony. Not this time anyway.

I brushed my teeth, contemplating the marvel of hearing the Voice speak audibly. Poignant phrases echoed in my spirit: *Pray 'Lord, change me'...Serve Dony as if he was Christ...Would you like Me to send you the Helper?*

————— ·⸛·~· —————

GOLDEN STEPPING STONE
*Let Holy Spirit walk with you
through everyday life.*

————— ·⸛·~· —————

I finished my clean-up routine and entered the walk-in closet.

What should I wear today?

Instantly, I sensed a holy Form standing beside me.

Isn't it amazing...you can decide what you wear.

My pounding heart, flushed face, and jellied knees testified that my Heavenly Father had sent Holy Spirit, the Helper, just like He promised.[1] Being a spiritual giant, I responded eloquently.

Uh-huh.

Why don't you wear the red outfit?

The red one?

I sorted through my clothes.

I haven't worn that one in months.

Sometimes desperation will lead you to obedience. Feeling a little awkward, I donned the outfit Holy Spirit had suggested.

Hmmm. This is Dony's favorite.

Occasionally, you pray to see angels or Jesus or some heavenly vision. But when it really happens, what are you supposed to do?

Freak out?

Pray?

Fast?

Join a monastery?

Write a best-seller about the experience?

Get an agent?

Book yourself on TBN?

Somehow there was a knowing deep inside...Holy Spirit wanted to walk with me through my everyday life. I wasn't sure how long He would be with me as tangibly as this, but I decided to go with the flow.

I headed for the kitchen to make coffee. He went with me.

Why don't you make pancakes and sausage?

Pancakes and sausage? I haven't made them in months.

Obediently, I dug through the pantry and freezer for the needed ingredients.

Hmmm. Pancakes and sausage are Dony's favorite.

It dawned on me. I had strange and unusual ways of punishing my husband.

Refusing to dress to please him.

Never taking time to prepare his favorite meals.

Selectively withholding sex.

The silent treatment.

These were all subtle ways I maintained some semblance of control. Holy Spirit's presence with me was enough to reveal the true issues buried in my heart.

I hated what I saw.

I hated that He made me see it.

I hated the knowledge that this was only the beginning of a long process.

I hated myself for ever praying, "Lord, change me."

I hated the fact that this was probably the only way out.

I hated that He knew what I was hating.

What Are You Wearing?

Someone said, "Clothes make the man." They probably don't "make" him, but they sure can convince him of who he is. A specific mind-set comes with what you wear.

A policeman dons a starched, official uniform, shiny brass badge, holstered gun, and riot baton not only to display his authority, but also to remind himself of his sworn duties to uphold the law. He projects an unmistakable air of authority.

An artist arms himself with a white cotton smock, a tilted beret, sable brushes, and a lagoon-shaped palette to stimulate his creativity, splashing his imagination to life on a stretched canvas. An artistic atmosphere awakens a sleeping artist inside.

An actor wears elaborate Elizabethan costumes to play Henry VIII...a space suit to play an astronaut...a wig with twenty-foot long tresses to play Repunzel. Can you imagine Cyrano de Bergerac without a six-inch nose? Outer wardrobe can almost convince the actor's heart that he is whom the apparel implies.

Not in the Mood

A woman "not in the mood" crawls into bed early with pink sponge hair-rollers, blue mud face mask, ratty old flannel nightgown, striped tube socks, rubbed down with Vicks, reading up on her Sunday school quarterly, and munching on a red onion sandwich.

The message?

"Don't even think about messin' with me tonight, Mister..."

But if she makes a candle-lit entrance to the *Greatest Hits* of Luther Vandross, Barry White or Johnny Mathis, floating on a cloud of see-through chiffon negligee, six-inch stilettos, atomized with Chanel Number 5, face made-up for *Glamour Shots*, carrying a plate of raw oysters in one hand and a bottle of massage oil in the other...

The message?

"Better brace yourself, Mister!"

What you wear sends a definite message. To you and everyone.

Blind Bartimaeus

M ark 10:46-52 records a familiar story:

As Jesus was leaving town, trailed by His disciples and a parade of people, a blind beggar by the name of Bartimaeus, son of Timaeus, was sitting along-side the road. When he heard that Jesus the Nazarene was passing by, he began to cry out, "Son of David, Jesus! Mercy, have mercy on me!" Many tried to hush him up, but he yelled all the louder, "Son of David! Mercy, have mercy on me!" Jesus stopped in His tracks. "Call him over." They called him. "It's your lucky day! Get up! He's calling you to come!" **Throwing off his coat,** *he was on his feet at once, and came to Jesus. Jesus said, "What can I do for you?" The blind man said, "Rabbi, I want to see." "On your way," said Jesus. "Your faith has saved and healed you." In that very instant he recovered his sight and followed Jesus down the road* (TM).

Notice the phrase, *"Throwing off his coat."*

In Jesus' time, daily wardrobe easily identified people.

Pharisees wore phylacteries—obtrusively large, ornate ceremonial leather boxes on the forehead and left arm—and long, flowing gowns, proclaiming their supposed religiosity.

"I'm religious, I'm important."

Roman soldiers wore inimitable red plumes on their helmets and impressive silver breastplates.

"I'm powerful, I'm invincible."

Blind beggars wore tattered rag coats that were as readily identifiable as white canes or seeing-eye dogs are today.

"I'm blind, I'm beggarly."

When Jesus called, blind Bartimaeus was so confident he was going to be healed, he threw off his coat—representing his old identity which he was familiar with and accustomed to—and made a quantum leap of faith and received a new, healed identity.

Wearing Old Hand-Me-Downs?

Sometimes we wear "hand-me-downs." Word curses, if you will. Here are some of the most familiar ones I've heard repeated over and over again.

"My father died from a massive heart attack. I'll probably have heart problems too."

"Grandma wasn't married when she had Mama. Mama had me out of wedlock. I'll probably get knocked up too."

"All of our family has been on welfare for years. Can't get a good job if we tried. And if we do get a job, we can't keep it for more than a couple of weeks."

"Never had nothing...never will."

Sound familiar?

Very likely, Bartimaeus didn't choose his garment. Somebody else put it on him. But when Jesus came into his life, he made a choice to throw off the facts and enrobe himself with the Truth.

The Facts: he was a blind beggar.

The Truth: Jesus came on the scene to heal his past and restore his destiny.

Notice that Bartimaeus didn't just sit on the sidelines while his Answer passed him by.

He was too desperate to stay in the place of no vision and not enough.

He wouldn't be silenced by the masses and miss his miracle.

He did something positive and pro-active.

He cried out for help.

He threw off his pride.

He jumped up and made his way to Jesus.

So many people act like they are helpless victims who can't—or won't—do anything about their miserable lives. I have good news for you: *It's time to experience the divine exchange.*

The Divine Exchange

Are you wearing a filthy garment you chose—or somebody else picked out and put on you? Throw it off! Put on the garment of praise for the spirit of heaviness.

123

Holy Spirit began to show me that I had been wearing a "victim's robe." My appearance...my gestures...my conversations...my attitude...all conveyed the obvious message: *"Poor me. Please feel sorry for me. My life is pathetic. Please feel sorry for me. I'm a victim. Please feel sorry for me."*

Every day when I wake up, I may not be able to control all the circumstances in my life, but I can determine my attitude and responses.

I decide what I wear. I can wear a victim's robe or a victor's crown.

Need an oil change?

Take the oil of joy for mourning.

Covered in sackcloth and ashes?

Try beauty instead of ashes. (See Isaiah 61:3.) Experience the divine exchange!

*Clothe yourselves therefore, as God's own chosen ones (His own picked representatives), [who are] purified and holy and well-beloved [by God Himself, **by putting on** behavior marked by] tenderhearted pity and mercy, kind feeling, a lowly opinion of yourselves, gentle ways, [and] patience [which is tireless and long-suffering, and has the power to endure whatever comes, with good temper]....and above all these, [put on] love and enfold yourselves with the bond of perfectness [which binds everything together completely in ideal harmony]* (Colossians 3:12,14).

———— ·‿ ⌣· ————

GOLDEN STEPPING STONE
Practice the divine exchange.
Exchange your victim's robe
for a victor's crown.

———— ·‿ ⌣· ————

When I was a little girl, my mother always warned me, "Make sure you wear clean underwear. You never know...you may need to go to the hospital and you wouldn't want to be embarrassed."

Now that I'm older, I've chuckled at Mother's psychological ploys to make sure I had on clean barumbas.

Wonder if Aunty Em did the same thing to Dorothy?

Inside and Out

Some of us wear beautiful garments on the outside. We are like well-dressed mannequins. We look right. We say the right words. We've got the motions down pat. But underneath our façade—something's not quite right and only we know it.

Our hearts are impure.

Our motives are tainted.

Our thoughts are perverted.

Our hands are unclean.

Don't be like Naaman (see 2 Kings 5) who was attired in wealthy, regal robes but decimated inside. A leper swaddled in rags underneath silk finery.

Be willing to do whatever it takes to be whole and authentic. If it means dipping seven times in the Jordan—go ahead and do it.

Let the water of the Word wash you and make you clean—inside and out.

...cleansed...by the washing of water with the Word...in glorious splendor, without spot or wrinkle or any such things...[...holy and faultless] (Ephesians 5:26-27).

Everything [Christ] does and says is designed to bring the best out of her, dressing her in dazzling white silk, radiant with holiness (Ephesians 5:27 TM).

Don't you think it's time for a wardrobe change? Put on praise. Put on love. Put on the full armor of God.

And don't forget to change your underwear.

Endnotes

1. John 14:16-17,26 NASB "I will ask the Father, and He will give you another Helper, that He may be with you forever; that is the Spirit of truth, whom the world cannot receive, because it does not see Him or know Him, but you know Him because He abides with you, and will be in you....But the Helper, the Holy Spirit, whom the Father will send in My name, He will teach you all things, and bring to your remembrance all that I said to you."

Words satisfy the mind
as much as fruit does the stomach;
good talk is as gratifying as a good harvest.
Words kill,
words give life;
they're either poison or fruit—
you choose.[1]

Chapter 11

GOD'S OXYGEN

What is it about aromas?

Fresh baked bread. Grandpa's Old Spice. Vanilla beans. New-mown hay. Babies' bottoms. Raspberry Jell-O. Christmas garlands. German sauerkraut. Lifebuoy. Limburger cheese. Parson's Sudsy Ammonia. Exotic gardenias. Boys' locker rooms. Nail polish remover. Puppies' breath. Sanitized hospitals. Southern fried chicken. Starbucks. Brand new Mercedes Benz. Ocean mists.

Pancakes and sausage.

Now that'll wake up a drunk man!

I felt Dony coming down the hallway to the kitchen.

Love to have been a fly on the wall when he woke up in that bed full of Bibles.

I chuckled softly.

Wonder if he felt like a modern day Gulliver?

Holy Spirit just shook His head and smiled with me. The sheepish, puzzled expression on Dony's face said it all.

"Good morning, sweetheart!" I beamed cheerfully.

Wait a minute! Did I say that? Or did June Cleaver, Donna Reed, and Carol Brady all take possession of my body? Was this 'The Twilight Zone' or was I smoking poppies from Oz?

Dony peered at me sideways and mumbled hoarsely, "Uh...good morning" as he plopped down into his favorite easy chair. I poured a steaming cup of fresh brewed coffee and handed him the morning newspaper. He eyed me suspiciously then sniffed the delightful aromas wafting through the room.

"Yep, pancakes and sausage," I confirmed, turning back to the pantry. "Thought you might enjoy them."

I selected an unopened jar of Mom McGuire's famous homemade blackberry preserves and started to twist the tightly secured lid when I felt Holy Spirit propelling me back around the counter and right into Dony's lap.

It was like an out-of-body experience!

I handed my bewildered husband the jar of preserves. "Darling, would you mind opening this for me?" I heard myself cooing. "I just can't seem to do it."

He accepted the jar and rolled his eyes in one of those "oh-you-poor-little-weak-woman!" looks.

As his hand strained to turn the pressure-cooker sealed lid, I found myself reaching up, squeezing his flexed biceps and chirping adoringly, "There's nothing like being in the arms of a strong man."

Yuk! Barf in a bag!

I wanted to stick a finger down my throat but the Helper arrested me.

Come on. Work it, girl!

Holy Spirit coached me enthusiastically.

You can do this.

Dony gave me one of those "who-are-you-and-what-have-you-done-with-my-wife?" looks.[1]

"Is it just me or is it hot in here?" Dony asked as he handed over the opened jar. I gave him a quick peck on the cheek and replied melodiously, "I'll go check the thermostat for you, Honey."

Suddenly, the moment froze in time as Holy Spirit un-blinded my eyes.

See how differently he's responding, Reebs? Normally the two of you would be at each other's throats over what happened last night...or you wouldn't be talking at all. See that thermostat?

Yes, Sir.

God moves by atmosphere. You set the thermostat—you control the climate by the words you speak.

Excuse me?

Psalm 22:3 makes it abundantly clear. God inhabits the praises of His people. He moves, He thrives, He functions, He performs in your praises.

Well, I praise Him.

It's not just vertical praise directed to God, Reebs. It's also horizontal praise to one another.

But Dony is such a jerk!

See? That is exactly what I AM talking about. Can you start seeing Dony as fearfully and wonderfully made?[2] There is something praiseworthy in everybody.

You must not know my husband.

Sometimes you have to call things that are not as though they were.[3] Remember, you picked him. There must have been something there.

The sound of whistling in the kitchen unthawed the moment. Dony always whistles when he's having a good day.

Okay. Praiseworthy. Got it!

I hurried to flip the last pancakes on the griddle.

131

"Nice tune, Dony," was about all I could come up with, but hey, that was a start. I placed steaming, heaping, aromatic platters of pancakes and sausage in front of him.

"Wow, this looks great!" Dony exclaimed appreciatively, cautiously taking my hand in his. "And so do you."

He had noticed!

Holy Spirit gave me one of those "see-I-told-you-so" smiles.

God Moves by Atmosphere

*D*on't you hate smog?

Residents of industrialized cities constantly contend with the choking, black haze of pollution generated by enormous populations. Smog stings the eyes, blackens the lungs, clogs the pores with sooty grime, limits long distance vision, and filters life-giving sunshine.

Smog is a breeding ground for depression and disease.

Shortly after my *Twilight Zone*/pancakes-and-sausage experience, I was back to my old habit of trudging through tar pits. It was such a struggle to break those deeply engrained habits[4] of seeing life through dark colored glasses...grumbling, murmuring, and complaining...predicting the worst rather than expecting the best.

One day I was talking with a close friend..."givin' forth a message" about Dony—doggin' him for all his problems, failures, and his generally being a world-class jerk.[5]

All of a sudden in a Holy Spirit flashback, I saw disturbing images of myself: something like black smog was spewing out of my mouth...my words reeked with negativity, doubt, and unbelief. Stinging accusations formed on my lips, spewed into the atmosphere, polluting with a dense, putrid haze. It was dark, ominous, and satanic.

At that moment, I realized I was helping form the black cloud Dony and I were living under.

God moves by atmosphere...you control the climate by the words you speak...

A bucket of ice-cold water smacked me in the face.

God inhabits the praises of His people. He moves, He thrives, He functions, He performs in your praises.

I had always thought of praise as something we did in church. Praise *to* God. But I suddenly grasped praise is not only vertical—it's horizontal too. Praise *for* others.

Praise is God's oxygen. It's simple: God inhabits praise. To Him and to others. Praise is a magnet for God.

Praise is God's idea. He is the One who created praise for our lips to speak (see Is. 57:19).

Anytime genuine praise is offered—vertically or horizontally—God is bound to show up. He inhales our praise-filled words, smiles, deeds, and gestures. He is pleased with our sacrifice, receives it and in return, He exhales new life back into the praiser.

I already knew about vertical praise, but this horizontal praise idea was new and challenging.

The following scenarios played like videos on the screen of my mind. Here's the setting: Husband returns home from hard day at work. He drops into his favorite recliner, elevates his aching feet, and unfolds the afternoon paper. All he wants is a few moments of peace and quiet.

The Smog Video: Wife enters, complaining.

"Thanks a lot for calling and letting me know you were gonna be home so late again!"

or

"Did you actually go to work dressed like that?..."

or

133

"You better go in there and do something about your rotten kids..."

The Effect: The atmosphere is polluted. There's a lack of oxygen. God can't breathe. He's outta there.

The Praise Video: Wife enters, smiling.

"Hi sweetheart. I can see you've had a long, rough day. Why don't you just relax and let me rub your neck..."

or

"The color of that shirt looks great with your eyes..."

or

"You're a wonderful father. I'm so glad I don't have to raise our children all by myself..."

The Effect: The atmosphere is clear and clean. There's lots of oxygen. God can breathe. He dwells there, inhaling and exhaling life.

Words satisfy the mind as much as fruit does the stomach; good talk is as gratifying as a good harvest. Words kill, words give life; they're either poison or fruit—you choose (Proverbs 18:20-21 TM).

A Little Child Shall Lead Them

*U*nfortunately, there are some lessons you have to learn more than once...

Years later, our youngest daughter, Destiny, had just turned two. Everybody knows the "terrible twos" syndrome. (What you say *is* what you get.)[6] Destiny was a strong-willed, energetic, rambunctious two-year-old. (Must have gotten it from her father...)

When you're in a music ministry traveling for hundreds of miles a day on a 40'x8' touring bus crowded with a dozen people, everyone's nerves get on edge. A peacemaker by nature, I was trying to keep Destiny quiet and every-body else happy. I wanted her to be "textbook perfect."

Have you ever seen the mother of a two-year-old who's had it? My jaw was clinched in the tight, strained grin/grimace of someone who's coming down the last big drop of a hair-raising roller coaster ride. My temple veins were popping out like our trumpet-playing buddy Phil Driscoll when he's blowing the highest notes possible.

I was not a pretty baby.

I heard myself screech through grinding teeth, "Destiny Rambo McGuire! You never mind your mother!"

Whoosh! Suddenly, the presence of God left our bus.

I hadn't realized God's presence was even on our bus until it left.

It's kind of like the anointing. You don't always know what it is—but you sure know what it ain't.

Even some of the usually clueless young people on our bus looked up with bewildered *"What just happened?"* expressions.

GOLDEN STEPPING STONE
Praise is God's oxygen.

I bolted into the tiny, airplane-sized bathroom, pulled down the commode lid and sat down bawling my eyes out. (Somebody had forgotten to change the roll of toilet paper so I just wiped my nose on the sleeve of my jogging suit. Again.)

I'm such a failure as a mother! God, don't leave me! What am I supposed to do?

Praise.

Praise? Okay, I can do that.

I lifted my hands and obediently tried to think of something nice to say to God. Can I be honest? It was feeble and pitiful.

No. Praise.

I kicked into my best prayer language. It was deader than four o'clock.

Praise.

About that time, my little daughter opened the bathroom door and stared up at me, her big eyes full of hurt and questioning.

"Destiny, you're such a wonderful little girl," I heard myself saying. "You always mind your mommy. Daddy and I are so proud of you."

Astonished, she looked at me and grinned, "Really?"

I drew her up in my arms, held her close and tickle-kissed her soft little neck. Suddenly the presence of God whooshed into the tiny cubicle with tangible force.

It was a Kodak moment.

Remember, Reebs. Praise is My oxygen.

How could I have forgotten? My words had been smog-filled...not praise-filled. My words had "killed"...not brought life. For the next few precious moments, Destiny and I snuggled and talked and played together. Then I carried my curly-headed little ballerina to her bunk and tucked her in for an overdue afternoon nap.

"Mommy, sing 'Can Do,'" Destiny mumbled sleepily. I stroked her back and quietly sang her favorite lullaby.

"I got a horse right here
His name is Paul Revere ...
Can do, can do
The horse says that Destiny can do..."[7]

While Destiny slept, I convened a group conference in the front of the bus. First of all, I repented for my negative words and actions, then shared my pancakes-and-sausage experience—how praise is God's oxygen. God moves by atmosphere.

I laid down the law. "From this point on, the only words spoken over Destiny or anyone on this bus will be praiseworthy."

Finally, brothers and sisters, whatever is true...worthy of respect...just...pure...lovely...commendable...if something is excellent or praiseworthy, think about these things (Philippians 4:8 NET).

Within two weeks, Dony and I had a changed daughter. And we had a happy bus.

———— ·ᴗ ᴗ· ————

GOLDEN STEPPING STONE
Words kill—words give life.
You choose.

———— ·ᴗ ᴗ· ————

You may be thinking, "Reba, this will never work in my situation. You don't know my spouse...or my children...or my boss..."

If you're willing to look deeply enough, there is something praiseworthy about everybody and every situation.

I'll remind you of what Holy Spirit spoke to me. Sometimes you've got to call the things that are not as though they were. You've got to call things that don't exist yet into being.

...God...who makes the dead live again and speaks of future events with as much certainty as though they were already past (Romans 4:17 TLB).

What's your thermostat setting? *Smog* or *Praise?*

Endnotes

1. Months later after he was powerfully delivered, Dony confessed to me that that Wednesday morning experience had felt like an Alfred Hitchcock thriller. When I snuggled into his lap, he halfway expected me to pull out a butcher knife and slice his throat. *Now why didn't I think of that?*

2. Psalm 139:14 KJV. "I will praise Thee, for I am fearfully and wonderfully made."

3. Romans 4:17b "...who gives life to the dead and calls those things which do not exist as though they did." (NKJV)

"...the God who makes the dead alive and summons the things that do not yet exist as though they already do." (NET)

"...God who gives life to the dead and who creates something out of nothing." (NCV)

4. Researchers have discovered it takes 21 days to form a new habit and 28 days to break an old one.

5. It is important to keep private arguments between you and your spouse private. The main problem with airing or venting to a friend is that you and your spouse will probably make up, but your friend will continue to remember the character assassination and hold your negativity against your spouse. Learn to keep private arguments private.

6. Thank you, Padre. (Padre is my name of endearment for one of my spiritual fathers, Rev. Don Gossett, who authored the best selling *What You Say Is What You Get*.)

7. "Can Do" from the Broadway musical *Guys and Dolls*. Written by Frank Loesser. Published by Hal Leonard Corp. Used by permission.

"Forgive Me"

Every day I give You reason to cry
I see the hurt in Your eyes
but stronger yet I see the love that shines
Help me learn to take on the nature of You
and love more than I accuse
and pardon others like You taught me to

Something happens inside my heart, Lord, when I obey
Something happens inside my heart every time I pray

Forgive me
as I learn how to forgive
the ones who broke my heart the way I've broken Yours
Forgive me
as I learn how to forgive and reach on out through the pain
and touch with hands of grace
Forgive me

As You prayed for those who crucified You
'Forgive, they don't know what they do'
Compassion reached out to a world confused
Help me learn to bless those who persecute me
and love all my enemies
and show them mercy like You've shown to me

Something happens inside my heart, Lord, when I obey
Something happens inside my heart every time I pray

Forgive me
as I learn how to forgive
the ones who broke my heart the way I've broken Yours
Forgive me
as I learn how to forgive and reach on out through the pain
and touch with hands of grace
Forgive me

Chapter 12

BOMB YOUR ENEMY

What is it about 3:00 in the morning?

I keep asking this question—but no one has given me a satisfactory answer yet.

Things were very erratic, volatile, and unpredictable between Dony and me. With Holy Spirit's help, I was learning to look for signs of improvement in our relationship. The oxygen of praise was gradually clearing the dense atmosphere in our home. At least the physical abuse had stopped. Thank God!

Dony was still drinking heavily. Still sleeping around. And to complicate matters more, not only was he still using illegal drugs himself, I suspected he was dealing them too.

One afternoon, I was cleaning out a seldom-used deep freeze in the garage. I didn't remember having so much stuff in there.

Hmmm. What are all these little packets anyway?

I always put labels on aluminum foil, but these were unmarked. I picked up the heftiest shiny bundle and peeled back one frosty layer after another.

What I unwrapped that day sure weren't hamburger patties...

My worst fears were confirmed as I sorted through shriveled stems of marijuana Dony had stashed in the bottom of our deep freeze.[1] An unmarked box on the shelf above the freezer contained what had to be thousands of dollars worth of cocaine, black pills, red pills...multi-colored pills of all sorts, shapes and sizes.

When Dony stumbled into the house late that night, wasted and drunk, I pretended to be asleep. I couldn't deal with him right then. I was angry, afraid, and disgusted. Thankfully, for once he left me alone and within a few minutes, he was snoring loudly.

By this time in our marriage, Dony was drinking a quart-and-a-half of vodka everyday...plus downing a variety of drugs. When he finally passed out at night, he was practically impossible to wake up. (I think he would have slept through the bombing of Hiroshima.) Desperation pushed me to do something—anything. I couldn't go on living like this.

What to do? Oil! That's what I need. Anointing oil. And lots of it!

I rushed to the kitchen pantry and unearthed a king-size bottle of Bertolli Extra Virgin olive oil.

Hmmm. At least something in our house is virgin.

Passing through the laundry room, I grabbed a couple of big beach towels and charged back to the bedroom armed for bear. Dony was dead to the world as I climbed onto the bed and rolled him over, tucking and spreading a towel underneath him.

This was fixin' to be messy and I didn't want to ruin my clean sheets.

"Dony's got the same problem as the Tin Man," I announced to Holy Spirit. "He needs some oil!"

I turned the gargantuan bottle upside down and started pourin' and prayin'. Pourin' and prayin'. Pourin' and prayin'.

It was amazing.

I had that pancakes-and-sausage anointing as I flipped over a greased-up-slicked-down-slippery-sopping Dony...tucked and spread the other towel and kept pourin' and prayin'. Pourin' and prayin'.

"You want pancakes, Dony McGuire? I'll give you pancakes!" I cackled maniacally.

I marinated his hair with oil, smearing the thick liquid into his scalp, beard, and eyebrows. Pourin' and prayin'. Pourin' and prayin'. If I added a little balsamic vinegar, I could have been sleeping with a tossed salad that night!

Just as I was about to drain the last of the oil, a strange wave of déjà vu washed over me.

Maybe I could pour the rest down his nose...kill him...and tell God he died!

Crazy tabloid headlines flashed before my eyes once again: *GOSPEL GRAMMY WINNER DIES MYSTERIOUSLY IN BED—BAPTIZED BY BERTOLLI?...ASPHIXIATED BY ANOINTING OIL?...MUZZLED BY MAZZOLA?...TRAUMATIZED TIN MAN TERMINATED?...GAGGED BY GREASING?*

Once again, the possibilities were endless.

Warfare! That's what I've gotta do. Spiritual warfare. And lots of it!

I dove off the bed, oil dripping from my hands, and marched around the bed singing "Onward, Christian

Soldiers" at the top of my lungs. I commandeered the television remote control and made it my drum major baton.

Four verses later, I remembered something about "warfare prayer"...so I slapped on some war paint and launched into the most fervent hullabaloo since my Cherokee ancestors danced around campfires.

I was bindin' and I was loosin'. I was hackin' and I was spewin'. I was renouncin' and I was rebukin'.

It was amazing.

Holy Spirit was just standing there by the bed. Silent. I think He was in shock. I certainly hadn't asked His opinion about my "new ministry," but I was quite sure He approved.

This is great, isn't it?

Why don't you just tithe and God will rebuke the devourer for your sake?

Excuse me?

You are trying to do His job. Your job is to be obedient with the Lord's tithe.

But Dony won't let me tithe. I don't know any drug dealers who would.

I'm not talking about Dony. I'm talking about you. YOU tithe on what you steward.

You mean the little household money Dony gives me every week?

Reebs, the tithe from your "little household money" becomes a bomb in the hand of God to destroy the works of the enemy against you.

A bomb?

Yes, a bomb. Do you want to see Dony change? Do you want the devourer rebuked for your sake? Then tithe.

Why didn't You tell me that before?

You didn't ask.

144

Put a Bomb in God's Hands

*H*ave you ever felt like everything you touch blows up?

The dishwasher breaks down for the third time in a month.

The kids are chronically sick and have to be taken to the doctor all the time.

The day after the warranty runs out on your car, the transmission drops out.

What's wrong?

Why is everything going against you?

In our ministry, we deal with a lot of people with problems like these. After listening for a few minutes, among other questions, I generally ask, "Are you a consistent tither?"

Ninety-nine percent of the time, the answer is "No."

Not tithing is at the root of so many problems. Examine this passage of Scripture and you'll see what I mean.

> Will a man rob or defraud God? Yet you rob and
> defraud Me. But you say, In what way do we rob or
> defraud You? [You have withheld your] tithes and
> offerings. You are cursed with the curse, for you are
> robbing Me, even this whole nation. Bring all the
> tithes (the whole tenth of your income) into the store-
> house, that there may be food in My house, and
> prove Me now by it, says the Lord of hosts, if I will
> not open the windows of heaven for you and pour
> you out a blessing, that there shall not be room
> enough to receive it. And I will rebuke the devourer
> [insects and plagues] for your sakes and he shall
> not destroy the fruits of your ground, neither shall
> your vine drop its fruit before the time in the field,

says the Lord of hosts. And all nations shall call you happy and blessed, for you shall be a land of delight, says the Lord of hosts (Malachi 3:8-12).

It is not my intention to get into a heavy-duty dissertation about the tithe. I just want to share with you a few principles that have changed our lives.

Early on in our walk with God, we were taught a valuable lesson that the tithe is marked for destruction.[2] One of the Hebrew words associated with the tithe is *charam*, which translates "marked to destroy...marked for destruction."[3]

In simple layman's terms: The tithe is like a ticking time bomb. You never know when or where it will explode. When we faithfully surrender the tithe and place it in God's hands, He uses it to destroy the enemy, the devourer. God literally blows up the schemes of the destroyer. That's one of the purposes of the tithe...to destroy the works of satan.

Destroying satan's works against us. Isn't that a great thought?

However, if we fail to surrender the Lord's tithe[4]—when it's in our hands—it's still going to blow up something. That something is usually us. Our lives. Our stuff.

————— ·‿ ‿· —————

GOLDEN STEPPING STONE
Put a bomb in the hands of God:
Tithe.

————— ·‿ ‿· —————

Maybe this is a new concept for you, but I've seen God use this one important principle to change the lives of thousands—including Dony's and mine.

I can hear someone ask, "Reba, is God after my money?"

No, God is after your poverty. He wants you blessed! Your obedience with the tithe will bring the blessing of God into every area of your life.

God is very fair—He has established the same standard for everyone. The same pathway to blessing: we don't *have* to tithe—we *get* to tithe! It is a privilege of sonship.

I can hear someone else whining, "I tried tithing and it didn't work for me..."

Tithing isn't something you "try" any more than salvation is something you try.

Imagine this scenario: A bridegroom is standing at the altar. His beautiful bride walks down the aisle and greets him. He takes her hand, looks deeply into her eyes and says, "You know, we're gonna 'try' this for 90 days and see if it works..." That bride would probably throw her bouquet in his face and march right back up the aisle and out of his life.

You don't "try" marriage. It's a commitment based on love and covenant. Tithing is a similar commitment. For better or worse. For richer or poorer. In sickness and in health.

When I began to tithe on my little household money, the Lord used it to fight my battles against the devil. All my "oil and warfare" efforts were insignificant compared to what God could do through my obedience with the tithe. I learned to tithe in faith because what is not of faith is sin.[5] It misses the mark. The Lord also taught me to tithe cheerfully, joyfully...and not see my giving as loss.[6]

The highest form of faith is trust. When we tithe in faith, cheerfully, joyously, obediently, we are saying to the Father, "We trust You. We believe You are going to stand behind Your Word. We believe in Your principles. We believe You are not a man that can lie.[7] We believe You are going to use the tithe to bomb our enemy!"

Endnotes

1. Incidentally, after two traumatic experiences with freezers, I finally gave mine away!

2. When Holy Spirit spoke to me about the tithe being like a bomb against the enemy, I understood enough to start taking a few baby-steps. Not long after Dony's miraculous deliverance, he delved deeper into the Scriptures and has received powerful revelations about the tithe. He has since preached these life-changing principles around the world, resulting in the windows of Heaven opening and unprecedented blessings overflowing.

3. *Strong's Exhaustive Concordance* (Iowa Falls, IA: World Bible Publishers, Inc., 1989), H2763, H2764.

4. Leviticus 27:30,32. "And all the tithe of the land...is the Lord's; it is holy to the Lord...And all the tithe...the tenth shall be holy to the Lord."

5. Romans 14:23 "....whatever does not originate and proceed from faith is sin."

6. 2 Corinthians 9:7 "Let each one [give] as he has made up his own mind and purposed in his heart, not reluctantly or sorrowfully or under compulsion, for God loves (He takes pleasure in, prizes above other things, and is unwilling to abandon or do without) a cheerful (joyous, 'prompt to do it') giver [whose heart is in his giving]."

7. Numbers 23:19 "God is not a man that He should lie; He doesn't change His mind like humans do. Has He ever promised without doing what He said?" (TLB)

"The Voice"

The Voice
beckons on the winds of relentless Grace
calling through the tangled webs of savaged concrete jungles
slicing through the razored opiate midnights
that camouflage themselves as great adventures
Yesterday's skeletons pretending to be heirlooms
crouching in shame-infested cesspools
Bony fingers poised on rusted triggers
Adept at hiding
Minute mites in rundown motel mattresses of cheap fear

It's a portable prison
Transported easily from the ghetto to The Opera
from kindergartens to old-folks homes
Loin-clothed beasts lurk in multiple disguises
of angel-dusted snow and black-light snakeskin corsets
Tarnished tongues
Slithering seductions
Licking lies
to polluted politicians
clinical clergy, haggard housewives
Wall Street wizards, radical rappers
and blue collar nine-to-fivers

Still...

The Voice calls[h]

Chapter 13

THE POPPY FIELD

What is it about hell on earth?

*I*t usually gets worse before it gets better.

Dony's behavior had grown more bizarre, paranoid, dangerous, and violent. I rejected repeated warnings of family, friends, and colleagues to leave him. In spite of their well-intentioned pleadings, I couldn't hear them. I felt powerless to leave him.

Why?

I had become as sick as Dony.

The basic credo of all 12-Step programs identifies alcoholism and drug addiction as a progressive "family" disease. Addiction infects everyone and affects everything it gets close to. However, this depiction doesn't begin to describe the debilitating, insufferable pain—the hideous death grip—the assassin's murderous plot to kill, steal, and destroy.[1]

Addiction ever so slowly paralyzes like seductive, poisonous clouds of black, blinding ink of a possessed monster-octopus. Its far-reaching, toxic tentacles patiently strangle the life force from its victims' body, emotions, sanity, relationships, productivity, finances, creativity, and spirituality.

Remember: addiction takes no prisoners.

Dony's addiction had progressed to a whole new dimension. He had become his own chemist, combining prescriptions scammed from four different doctors with all the illegal street drugs he could get his hands on. Reduced to skin-and-bones because he rarely ate well, his daily intake consisted of gallons of strong coffee, three packs of cigarettes, and occasional junk food. It wasn't unusual for him to wash down a handful of pills with half a bottle of vodka while smoking a joint and snorting cocaine.

I would love to say I was heroic Little Miss Spiritual Giant resplendent in flowing Kathryn Kuhlman gowns, but that's simply not the case. I was gradually slipping into insanity and Holy Spirit's tangible presence was waning. I am sure it was because He was so grieved with me for succumbing to the demon-bait luring me deeper into cesspools of sin along with Dony.

How could this happen?

After all, I had experienced face-to-face encounters with precious Holy Spirit. He had visited me personally and intimately. He had touched me profoundly, imparting supernatural wisdom and strategies to me every time I sought Him. Yet in spite of these mind-boggling manifestations and divine encounters, I found myself doing things I never dreamed I would do.

How do I distill my twisted reality into a single sentence?

There was no me left.

Hopelessness is a terrible thing. Hope deferred makes your heart sick[2]...spawning the "Oh well, if you can't beat 'em, join 'em" syndrome, plunging you to unspeakable despair. Without hope, there is no anchor for the soul, mind, will, and emotions.[3]

Like Bonnie and Clyde, you may not be the one who actually robs the bank, you just drive the getaway car. You may not pull the trigger, you simply ignore the growing arsenal of guns and ammunition. You become an accessory to the crime: by doing a little of what they do a whole lot...by compromising your once high standards in fruitless attempts to relate and fit in with the one you love.

I was too terrified to inhale razor-thin lines of cocaine, but I finally coughed my way through marijuana. I hated vodka, but eventually downed a whole bottle of wine now and then. I didn't have multiple affairs or one-night stands, but I was unfaithful to my marriage vows. I had collapsed, drowning in denial.

I was as morally bankrupt as my husband.

Alone one night, I mixed painkillers and decongestants with a shot-glass of B & B. In retrospect, I don't think I meant to kill myself—I just wanted to escape. I yearned to close my eyes and sleep peacefully for a very long time. Perhaps when I awoke, the nightmare would finally be over. Instead I came to in an intensive care unit with tubes forced down my throat and IVs stuck in both arms.

Sometimes Dorothy lies down in the scarlet poppy field on purpose.

The Haunted Forest

A near-death experience has a way of rallying the troops. While I was in the hospital, Dony vowed, "If you'll just live—I will get help..."

My parents insisted he live up to that promise.

Since we were basically ignorant of where to turn and the different types of treatment available, Dony chose a facility close to the house in a picturesque, mountainside setting.

This well-known program treats its patients using "aversion therapy." The program's approach is to force a paradigm shift from loving to loathing alcohol.

Dony entered a small, mirrored room which resembled a bar. Therapists impersonating bartenders poured him glass after glass of Stolichnaya, Dony's drink of choice, until he was loop-legged drunk. Then they administered medication which induced immediate physical reactions, extreme abdominal pain, violent vomiting, and profuse sweating. They required Dony to watch himself in the mirrors as he purged. The theory was to break his spirit with cruel, demoralizing tactics and sarcastic, demeaning ridicule.

Dony was breezing through the 21-day program with flying colors. After each Sunday afternoon Family Day visit, I drove back down the hillside, hopeful and expectant of my husband's victorious recovery.

Within two weeks of being discharged, Dony started making daily stops at the liquor store. (So much for aversion therapy.)

The next program he entered was a little better in that they worked the 12-steps more thoroughly. Upon his release, they prescribed a preventative drug, Antibuse. The patient using this drug is warned of the potentially dangerous side effects if liquor is ingested...the heart races wildly, the body heats abnormally, the skin turns blood red, the nausea is overwhelming.

Yep, you guessed it. We rushed a puking, poppy-red Dony to Emergency.

The forest was becoming more haunted, tangled, and impassable than ever.

Endnotes

1. John 10:10 "The thief 's purpose is to steal, kill and destroy. My purpose is to give life in all its fullness." (TLB)

2. Proverbs 13:12 "Hope deferred makes the heart sick; but when dreams come true at last, there is life and joy." (TLB)

3. Hebrews 6:19 "This hope we have as an anchor of the soul, a hope both sure and steadfast..." (NASB)

"Wounded Soldier"

See all the wounded
Hear all their desperate cries for help
Pleading for shelter and for peace
Our comrades are suffering
come let us meet them at their need
Don't let a wounded soldier die

Come let us pour the oil
Come let us bind the hurt
Let's cover them with the blanket of His Love
Come let us break the Bread
Come let us give them rest
Let's minister healing to them
Don't let another wounded soldier die

Obeying their orders
they fought on the frontlines for the King
capturing the enemy's strongholds
Then weakened from battle
satan crept in to kill their life
Don't let a wounded soldier die

Come let us pour the oil
Come let us bind the hurt
Let's cover them with the blanket of His Love
Come let us break the Bread
Come let us give them rest
Let's minister healing to them
We can't let another wounded soldier die[i]

Chapter 14

THE CASTLE DUNGEON

What is it about trap doors?

One Tuesday afternoon as I was leaving acting class, my coach pulled me aside. "Are you okay? You look like hell."

If he only knew.

Dony was waiting for me when I got home. He was blazing drunk, livid, crazy, in my face for hours at a time. The next three days, his barbaric, psychological mind-games escalated to insufferable new heights.

The pain in my soul was agonizing and overwhelming.

I had no anger to fight back with.

No voice to beg with.

No mental prowess to bargain with.

If only I could click my heels three times and be back in Ma Rambo's quilt closet! Safe from the monsters in the night. My haven. My hiding place.

Instead, I crawled into my clothes closet, drowning in a tidal wave of yearning for Germs to come pounce on my chest and lick away my tears.

But Germs was long gone. So was Ma. So was my childhood. My innocence. My marriage. My dreams.

Plunging headfirst into a bottomless pit of despair and loss, I reached for my heaviest winter coat and curled into a fetal position on the floor.

Ah. Yes, there it was. The black abyss. My familiar darkness.

I don't know how much sand trickled through the ensorcelled hourglass. Chained in my closet dungeon by flying monkey demons, I wasn't sane enough to track the hours.

⁘

In ironic role-reversal, Dony eventually dragged my lethargic frame onto the bed, irritated because there was nothing left for him to toy with.

He got drunker.

Higher.

Didn't leave the house.

Didn't pick up phone calls.

Didn't answer the doorbell.

Reba's note: Up to this point in our saga, I have intentionally focused on Dony and me as the principle players. Because the following events are largely a blur to me, my family and Judy have filled in the blanks. I think a survival mechanism kicked in and my brain went into overload to cope.

Could It Get Any Worse?

Judy didn't think much of it when Reba failed to answer the phone on Tuesday night. But when she missed an important lunch meeting the next day, Judy drove by the house to check things out. Nobody answered the door, so she used the spare key and came in.

"Hello!" she called. "Anybody home?"

Glancing down the hall to the kitchen, she saw broken glass on the floor. The refrigerator door ajar. An empty coffeepot smoldering. As she doused the scalded decanter under running water, she noticed him out of the corner of her eye.

Dony was slumped over his desk in a drunken stupor, still grasping an empty bottle of Vodka. Two 24-track recording tape boxes lay open in plain view. One was filled with dozens of pills of every color in the rainbow, charred metal pipes, and crystallized lumps of God-knows-what. The other box contained dried stalks of marijuana, a cigarette rolling machine and packets of ZigZag papers. Now she understood why Dony had always insisted on keeping his tape masters on a bookshelf in his office instead of in a temperature-controlled vault. They were decoys for his stash of drugs.

"Dony, are you okay?" Judy posed, tentatively touching him on the shoulder. "Reba and I were scheduled for a meeting today and she didn't show up. What's going on?"

Dony rose up slowly, scowling, wiping his mouth on the back of his hand. "She's in bed. Not feeling good."

"I'll go check on her."

"No! I've got everything under control. I don't want you bothering her. Just let her sleep."

"Are you sure? Maybe I'll just peek in and see if she needs anything."

"I said...I've got everything under control. Just leave her alone!"

Dony was in another one of his foul rages. From previous experience, Judy knew pressing him any further would only make matters worse for Reba. Reluctantly, she got back in the car, shaking her head in sadness and disbelief.

On Thursday, she brought by some chicken soup as an excuse to check on her friend. Dony's car wasn't in the driveway so she headed straight for the master bedroom.

Huddled, eerily motionless under a pile of blankets, Reba didn't respond when she turned on the lights. She slowly pulled back the covers, revealing a disheveled, lethargic, dehydrated Reba.

"Oh my God! What in the world's going on?" Judy demanded. "You look like death!"

With one finger, she lifted a matted lock of hair. Reba stirred slightly. Her skin was a sickly, gray-green pallor. Something was definitely wrong. Visions of Reba's near overdose a few months earlier alarmed Judy.

"Did you take anything you shouldn't have?" she asked with mounting concern.

"No," Reba mouthed through parched, cracked lips.

"This is ridiculous. I'm calling your dad."

"No...I'll be alright."

"You're not alright! What's going on with you and Dony?"

"Shhhhh. Don't yell. He'll hear you."

"He's not even home. Listen to me, Reba Faye, you've gotta get away from that man. This is insane!"

Judy dialed Reba's father and quickly summarized the situation. Reba took the phone as her father pleaded for her to listen to reason.

"We'll work it out, Dad. We always do," she defended, listlessly handing the phone to Judy.

"Buck, I don't care what she says," Judy insisted. "If you could see what I'm looking at right now, you would be outraged! I think you need to come and get her. You're the only one who can."

Hanging up the phone, Judy announced, "Your father is on his way and will be here in 20 minutes. Come on, let's get you ready."

Reba started to protest, "Jude, I told you we'll be okay," and paused mid-sentence.

Get out of the house now. This time he's going to kill you.

Somehow The Voice resonated above the roar. Somehow there was strength enough to obey.

Escape

"Just throw my make-up in an overnight bag. Clean pajamas are in the bottom drawer," Reba croaked weakly. "I'd help you but I don't think I can walk."

"You don't have to do anything," Judy assured, carefully daubing Reba's face with a damp cloth.

Grabbing Judy's forearm with a growing sense of urgency, Reba whispered, "We've got to hurry before Dony gets back!"

Something in her voice frightened Judy and propelled her into overdrive.

Within minutes, Buck Rambo charged into the house. He took one look at his daughter lying in the bed and said in sad, broken tones, "Your mother's getting your room ready."

He picked up Reba's frail body in a swooping motion. Wrapping her arms around his neck, she sighed with relief and resignation. He carried her like a little child to the car, calling over his shoulder, "Judy, can you handle the bags?"

"No problem. You go on," she replied. "I'll be right behind you as soon as I close up the house."

Buck gingerly placed his daughter into the front seat, leaned down and tenderly kissed her swollen cheek. "Come on, Honey. Let's go home."

"...And Suddenly the Hinges Started to Unhitch..."

*D*ony was experimenting with new combinations of drugs. An evil force was driving him to greater violence and insanity. Even he knew he was over the edge.

He was outraged to return to an empty house, realizing someone—somehow—had helped Reba escape. She was entirely too weak to leave under her own steam.

"You think you're gonna leave **me**?" Dony thundered at the silver-framed picture on his nightstand. It was Reba's latest publicity photo. She was wearing a beautiful designer gown he had purchased.

Seized with a psychotic urge, he defiantly mocked the image, "I think you forgot something..."

He kicked open the closet door, loaded his arms with Reba's clothes and bolted out the front door. Storming down the driveway into the cul-de-sac, he hurled the garments onto the black asphalt with explosive force.

"I'll show you!" he laughed derisively, energized by mounting insanity. He carted out armload after armload, leaving a telltale path from the bedroom all the way to the growing pile in the street.

Not one neighbor said a word. In Los Angeles, no one dared.

*H*alfway to the Rambos', Judy suddenly remembered, "Jewelry! I forgot Reba's jewelry!" She turned the car around and headed back to the house, muttering, "I better go get it before Dony hocks it!"

Racing up the street to the cul-de-sac, Judy suddenly slowed down and gawked at the unbelievable sight of Reba's beaded stage gowns, rhinestoned pumps, exquisite hats, feathered capes and expensive furs...strewn carelessly across the front lawn... and heaped unceremoniously in the street with jeans, shirts, sweaters, boots, shoes, purses, belts and coats. Just as she pulled into the driveway and parked next to Dony's red convertible, he blustered out of the house laden with more cargo of vengeance.

"Have you lost your mind or what?" she yelled as she got out of the car, picking up a discarded shoe.

"Where is she?" Dony snarled ominously. "Where did you take her?"

"You think I'm telling you when you're in this condition? No way!"

"She's my wife! You better tell me where she is!!"

Adrenaline pumping, he yanked Judy by the jacket and flung her onto the hood of his car.

"Damn you, Dony McGuire! You crazy drunk! Get out of my face or I'll kill you!"

Infuriated, she drew up one leg and kneed him in the gut, shoving him forcefully backwards. Off balance, he stumbled awkwardly against the garage door.

"Reba's gone and she's not coming back!" Judy screamed as she slid off the hood, straightening her jacket.

"You tell me where she is now...or I'll kill you!"

Aware that he was fully capable of keeping his word, she conceded angrily, "Her dad came and got her."

Dony stomped back toward the house.

"Get outta here and don't ever come back!" he warned, kicking the front door open. "I'm gonna get my wife back!"

Judy hurriedly rescued an armload of Reba's clothes from the cul-de-sac, dumped them in a back bedroom and grabbed the jewelry bag.

She had never been so glad to get outta Dodge.

"Prodigal"

The smell of sin and death
strangles my throat and makes me dizzy
Rotting flesh
Decaying dreams
Coffined confidence
Pigpen piranhas nibble on my soul
and demons dance
as I sink further
into the scorpion-infested quick sand

Guilt screams in my ears
like a thousand run-away trains
Relentless sirens of mocking madness
sucking sanity through a cesspool straw
Distorted images spin wildly
Torturing, mocking, savage beasts

In the midst of the tornado
Somewhere...
There is a whispered Word
A shadowy Figure

Reaching through the
C
y
c
l
o
n
e

Chapter 15

WHAT'S LOVE GOT
TO DO WITH IT?

～ Reba ～

*What's love got to do with it,
got to do with it?*[1]

This time I was done. This time something had shut down inside me. When the Voice warned, ***"Get out. This time he's going to kill you"***...I translated, "It's over. You're free! You can get divorced now."

Isn't it funny how we hear?

In the safety of my parents' home, I slept for days as they nurtured me back to health. They treated me like I was their little five-year-old again. Actually, it was very sweet.

Mother brought in stunningly arranged bed trays heaping with her delicious gourmet fare. I was so weakened and frail, she actually spoon-fed me.

167

Dad's answer to everything is a hot fudge sundae. Reduced from my normal size eight to size four, it was the first time in my adult life I could actually indulge without guilt. Even when I had no appetite, I could always eat ice cream.

Go figure.

My parents too were through with Dony. My 6'3" father had instilled such a fear of God—and of himself—Dony didn't even try to come around their home.

Fear can be a wonderful thing.

Still in survival and isolation mode, I wasn't taking phone calls from anyone. Dad screened Dony's relentless calls and wouldn't allow him to talk to me. It finally got so bad that Dad threatened to get a restraining order if Dony didn't stop harassing me. But when the phone rang at 2:00 one morning, I instinctively grabbed the receiver to keep from disturbing Mother and Dad.

Yep, it was a drunk-out-of-his-mind Dony. He pleaded, whined, cajoled, and needled, trying to win me back.

"You gotta come home. I really need you," he whimpered. "I promise...I've really changed. You know I would never hurt you, baby."

Yeah, right. I could hear how much he had changed.

Same slurred speech.

Same selfish demands.

Same self-pity.

Same old lies.

Same old same old.

"There's no way in hell I'll ever go back to you, Dony McGuire," I vowed emphatically. "The only way you'll ever see me again is in court."

"I'm just gonna kill myself," he moaned dramatically. "I can't live without you."

I was so sick of his theatrics. This was beginning to read like a low-budget B movie. Not only was the script bad, the actors stunk too.

For the first time in my life, Dony didn't move me at all.

"You know I've got a gun. I'm gonna end it all right now..." he snotted. "Tell Dionne I love her..."

·◡ ◞·

He's not going to kill himself. (My ears have a way of opening to The Voice at the craziest times.)

·◡ ◞·

"*Did* you hear me, Reba. I mean it. This time I'm really gonna do it!"

"Well...if that's what you think you've gotta do," I replied calmly.[2]

Sure enough—the gun fired with a loud explosion. His phone dropped and banged noisily against the side of his mahogany desk. Then silence.

He ain't dead.

(The Voice still speaks hillbilly to me.)

I hung up the phone, took the receiver off the hook and buried it under a mound of pillows to stifle the dull drone of dial tone. Plumping my pillow, I lay back down and proceeded to fall asleep. I got a great night's rest...and a supposedly dead Dony kept getting a busy signal all night long.

There is some justice in life.

Behind Bars

By this time, Dony had burned bridges with just about everybody. Our record company. Our manager. Our accountants. Our lawyers. Our band and singers. Our closest friends. Even his own family back in Oklahoma. Everybody was fed up with his lies, inconsistencies, manipulation, borrowing money, ranting and raving.

One night, he was arrested for drunk driving and thrown in jail. He called me to post bail but I didn't believe him. He had cried wolf so many times before.

Once again Ma Bell was buried under pillows.

After he wasted his one phone call, guards threw him in a big holding cell with dozens of other men. Dony was so loaded, he passed out for several hours until a rude wake-up call came in the form of a skid row derelict taking a leak all over him. Cold, nauseous, haggard, craving a fix, reeking with somebody else's urine, Dony couldn't believe it had come down to this.

He–Dony McGuire–was behind bars!

The final straw was a huge, leather clad biker and his hungry-eyed cohorts whistling and talking trash to him. Their intentions were very clear. Dony yelled for help and a duty guard had compassion.

"One more phone call, McGuire, but that's it," he warned gruffly.

This time Dony got through to our secretary and her husband who reluctantly drove down to City Jail and posted bail.

Wouldn't you think Dony would head to the nearest treatment center? Nope. That would make too much sense.

He drove straight home to an unopened case of Stolichnaya and tape boxes filled with drugs. He settled back behind his mahogany desk and got down to business.

What's Love Got to Do With It?

The business of getting high and numb and wild and crazy, that is.

For the next three days and nights, he didn't eat. Bathe. Shave. Sleep. He even gave up trying to phone people.

For those three days and nights, he drank. Smoked. Snorted. Mixed lethal concoctions of drugs. Ingested everything he could think of.

Dony was defying death.[3]

From the pit of hell itself,
Apollyon cued
"Requiem of the Damned in D Minor"

Liar hissed and spat the vile orchestrations
onto scorched parchment

Master conductor, Baal/Shame,
tapped his twisted baton
with cruel, resonating dominance

The hordes of hell snapped to attention
as the venomous, deafening overture swelled

Suicide played the hypnotic panpipe
of a luring snake charmer

The tympani of Torment punctuated the sinister score
featuring a diabolic dirge droned by Insanity and Fear
followed by a shrill solo screeched by Accusation.

Volcanic Fury mesmerized with odious crescendos,
sucking its victim to the hell-red edge of no return
teetering precariously high above the Lake of Fire[4]

Dony was tumbling headlong down his own jagged mountainside towards the black abyss called Hopelessness, about to be buried alive by the avalanche of netherworld voices, when the rope of Truth dropped into his battered heart.[5]

"What can wash away my sin?"[6]

From the deepest recesses of his soul, he heard his godly mother wooing him with an old, nearly forgotten song.

"Nothing but the Blood of Jesus!"

And the hordes of hell were instantly silenced as they dove under their orchestra chairs.

 "What can make me whole again?"

"How could I ever be whole again?" Dony shuddered.

"Nothing but the Blood of Jesus!"

Jesus? The Taskmaster?

His mind's eye returned to a frightening Sunday school picture of a violent Jesus driving out the money-changers from the Temple in Jerusalem. That kind of Jesus would never forgive him.

"O! precious is the flow
That makes me white as snow
No other fount I know
Nothing but the Blood of Jesus!"

The Taskmaster image melded into an inviting picture of the Gentle Shepherd reaching over a cliff to rescue a frightened lamb caught in a thicket.

Dony wasn't sure which—if any—Jesus would ever show Himself to a messed-up sinner like him. Deeply convicted, he laid his head on the cluttered desk and wept.

Even if He was gonna beat me up, I deserve it.

Suddenly he flashed back to a childhood vision experienced shortly after his leg was amputated.

He saw himself as a grown-up...preaching on a platform somewhere in Africa...wearing Bermuda shorts, of all things. In the vision, his leg was miraculously restored. A normal, whole leg with hair and everything. Muscles, calf, ankle, foot, and five toes. He was demonstrating to a huge crowd several of the artificial limbs he had worn before Jesus healed him.

As the scene unfolded, Dony had felt the unmistakable call of God on his young life and realized some day he would preach the gospel.

He hadn't thought about the childhood vision in many years.

Me? A preacher?

A preacher's supposed to be a man of God.

A man of integrity and influence like Billy Graham.

A man of passion and power like Oral Roberts.

He felt more like the prodigal son.

Talk about a pigpen! He was living in one.

His desk was worse than a slop-filled pig trough. Ashtrays heaped with endless cigarette butts and marijuana roaches. Dirty coffee cups with beige mold floating in

[handwritten: No one ever cared for me like Jesus]

[handwritten: Red if age]

the shallow dregs. Empty vodka bottles and drug paraphernalia glued with sticky scum rings onto the leather
blotter.

He was suddenly sickened and repulsed by the over-
powering stench of his own un-bathed body.

*You know it's bad when you can't stand the smell of your
own breath.*

His stomach growled insistently. *[handwritten: What a
lavish love]*

When was the last time I ate?

A thick stupor muddied his memory. A wave of profound sadness engulfed him. He had finally lost everything. He was terminally wasted, spent, and empty.

So this is what it means to hit bottom... *[handwritten: have in Jesus]*

Who could love a man in his condition? Who could
forgive him? Who would even want to?

[handwritten: all are sins + Gods + Bea]

"For my pardon, this I see
Nothing but the Blood of Jesus
For my cleansing, this my plea
Nothing but the Blood of Jesus!"

"Could He really clean me up?" Dony wondered.
Mom's soprano voice lifted the next refrain.

[handwritten: My God how Great thou art]

"This is all my hope and peace
Nothing but the Blood of Jesus
This is all my righteousness
Nothing but the Blood of Jesus!"

Never more grateful for his saintly mother, he clasped
his palms together in the prayer position learned by every
child around the world. Bowing his head for his first heartfelt prayer in years, his voice broke with deep emotion.

"Jesus, if You're really real..."

What's Love Got to Do With It?

No. He always knew Jesus was real.

Face glistening with tears, he cleared his throat and pleaded, "Jesus, I'm so sorry! If You can...if You will...please...help me."

Gust of Wind banished the slithering hordes of hell.

Sweet Aroma permeated the atmosphere.

Holy Presence walked right through the sliding glass doors, saturating the entire room with Glory and Light.

Jesus Christ, the Son of God, opened His arms in a wide, sweeping gesture of absolute acceptance.

Dony, I'm not mad at you. I only want to love you. I'm not here to beat the hell out of you. I'm here to love the hell out of you.

Dony's body trembled from the tangible pressure of His presence.

The love this Jesus offered him was intense and irresistible.

Too wonderful.

Too pure.

Too holy for someone as undeserving as he.

His heart was on the verge of imploding, bursting inwardly.

He couldn't bear any more!

Covering his face, he drew himself into a fetal position.

But that didn't stop this Jesus.

He walked right into Dony, consuming him with everlasting, unconditional Love.

At that same moment, Jesus stripped him of every ounce of drugs, alcohol, and foreign substances.

175

He was instantly sober.

Instantly delivered.

Instantly free.

Instantly filled with Holy Spirit.

Instantly in his right mind.

"And...he came to himself" (Luke 15:17 KJV).

Endnotes

1. Thank you, Tina.

2. Suicide threats are no joke. Contrary to popular belief, most people who commit suicide drop hints and leave clues because they do want help—they want someone to intervene in their hopelessness. Some have a chemical imbalance in the brain or are fighting what they perceive to be a losing battle against depression. Others are overwhelmed with the shame of addiction, sin, sexual perversion, etc.

I am not suggesting anyone take suicide threats lightly; however, in this particular situation, I had Holy Spirit's assurance Dony was just bluffing, trying to manipulate me. It was a smoke-screen, not a genuine threat. If someone you love threatens suicide, take it seriously and seek spiritual and professional counseling. (See Crisis Helpline information on pages 245-246.)

3. Reviewing the deadly combinations of drugs and alcohol Dony ingested during that final three-day binge, the doctors at the drug treatment facility in Atlanta later confirmed Dony should have died several times. It was only by the grace of God that he survived.

4. "Requiem of the Damned in D Minor" by Reba Rambo-McGuire and Judy A. Gossett. Copyright 2001. Used by permission.

5. See Chapter 3: "Life Before Oprah," p. 23.

6. "Nothing but the Blood of Jesus" by Robert Lowry. Public Domain.

**"The Prodigal
According to Reba"**

*People talkin' strange
you can't understand their language
you woke up cryin' in this crazy place
You're broke, you're tired and cold
and all your friends have left you
You're wondering how you ever got this low*

*But if you've left your harp hanging on the willow
Reach out, you still can strum a happy song
Brush the dirt off
pick up all the pieces
and get yourself on home where you belong*

*I'm sure you meant to fly to new heights
but somehow you landed on the floor
And now you've learned there's nothing greener
than the grass a-growin' 'round your own back porch*

*At home there's lots of love
there's a feast upon the table
they've got your slippers warmin' by the fire
So bundle up your pride and cast it to the four winds
but take instead the wisdom you've acquired*

*And if you've left your harp hanging on the willow
Reach out, you still can strum a happy song
Brush the dirt off
pick up all the pieces
and get yourself on home where you belong*[k]

Chapter 16

IF I ONLY HAD A HEART

What is it about a tin man who gets a new heart?

He will weep unashamedly—taking the risk of rusting—because he perceives the profound revelation: the same One who conferred his new heart also possesses an endless supply of oil.

Love. Grace. Mercy. Pardon.

Unchaining.

Healing. Restoration.

Infusion. Joy. Saturation.

A perfect heart.

The covenant of Peace. Nothing missing. Nothing broken.[1]

᷄ ᷄

My father has always been an early riser. Whether living on the rolling green hills of Kentucky or on the palm-lined boulevards of Beverly Hills...he has always loved mornings.

My parents had moved into the house once belonging to Hollywood legend Jean Harlow. Relaxing under the striped umbrella with a second cup of coffee and the *L.A. Times*, he glanced around at the lush tropical gardens, the carved marble statues, the shimmering, turquoise pool. As Dad counted his blessings, he smiled, feeling a little like Jed Clampett from *The Beverly Hillbillies*.

Life would be just about perfect if only Reba wasn't so miserable and brokenhearted.

He was startled when the phone rang.

Who's calling this early? Must be somebody from the East Coast who forgot the difference in time zones.

He reached for the cordless phone.

"Hello?"

"Dad?" Dony hesitated. "Hope I didn't wake you."

"No, I was just drinking in the California sunshine. Another miserable day in paradise," he chuckled softly. "What got you up so early?"

"That's what I need to talk with you about," Dony inhaled deeply. "Dad, last night I finally realized the mess I've created was all my own fault. The drinking. Drugs. Fooling around on Reba. Lying. Blaming everybody else...I don't know if you can understand, but I was teetering on the edge of hell...about to kill myself...when suddenly, I cried out to the Lord."

Dony never sounded this sober.

"Dad, I hope you can believe me...Jesus walked right into my office and told me He loved me. I didn't deserve it, but He loved me anyway." Dony's voice trembled. "Jesus didn't beat me up. He just forgave me and wiped the slate clean!"

As Dony described his encounter with Jesus, Dad was hearing more than words.

Something is definitely different.

180

"I know I don't have the right, but I need to ask a favor. Remember that treatment center in Georgia you and Mom told me about?"

Yeah, you cussed like a sailor when Dottie and I suggested you needed professional help.

"Well, I've been on the phone with them already this morning. There's a space open right now and they're willing to take me. I checked with the airlines and a non-stop flight is available this afternoon. Dad, I know Jesus has done something miraculous in me, but I'm still afraid to make the trip by myself."

Dony never admitted to being afraid of anything.

"I've got to find out the full extent of damage I've done to my body...and I need to get away from L.A. There are just too many things pulling on me here. I've got to get my head on straight. Would you consider going with me and making sure I get there okay? I don't know who else to call."

Why am I crying? Why do I still care about this messed up son-in-law who has tortured my baby girl?

You know truth when you hear it. Go with him.

"Alright, Dony. Come by here and we'll ride together to the airport," Dad agreed and added a firm warning, "but I'm not going to stay there and hold your hand. I'm catching the first flight back to L.A."

"That's okay, Dad. I can understand how you must feel. I'm just thankful you're even willing to make the trip with me."

⚬‿⚬

"Baby, are you awake yet?" my parents gently tapped on the bedroom door.

"Come on in," I croaked slowly, lazily stretching under the cool sheets.

"Here, Jebe. Drink this," Mother offered me a steaming cup of black coffee. As they sat down on the edge of my Victorian bed, I gratefully welcomed the morning brew, halfway propped myself on one elbow and instinctively leaned forward for one of Mother's famous "rub your back to wake you up" routines.

"Think you're alert enough to hear something important?" Dad posed. Shifting positions to better see his face, I drew a long sip of caffeine.

"Dony called this morning."

The familiar knot tightened in my stomach.

As Dad quietly related the essence of his early morning phone call, my cup clinked nervously against the delicate, bone china saucer.

"Jesus walked into his room? Yeah right! And I'm the Virgin Mary!" I scoffed nervously. "What was he smoking to come up with that one?"

"I know it sounds pretty farfetched, but I think something has happened to him," Dad affirmed.

"And you're buying that load of crap?!?" I fumed, bolting straight up in the bed.

I can't believe my own parents are so gullible.

"See! Dony's done it again! He's conned you! Can't you see he'll do anything to get me back?"

I was angry Dony was trying to sucker my father again.

I was angry he had the nerve to bring God into it.

I was angry he was pretending to want help.

I was angry he could still make me angry.

I was angry I was angry.

"Honey, this isn't about you right now. We know your mind is already made up," Mother reasoned. "This is about Dony. He needs help."

"If there's any chance of saving his life, I think this is it," Dad concluded. "I'd never forgive myself if something happened and I hadn't tried one last time."

"Okay, I can see you're gonna go through with this," I simmered. "But don't expect me to wave pom-poms and cheer you on..."

When Dony arrived to pick up Dad, I was astonished by his thin, pale, sunken appearance.

He'd lost even more weight since I left him.

He looked awful.

I was caught off guard when he didn't try to push or manipulate me. As he spoke with my parents, there was a strange brokenness about him.

In a moment of weakness, I almost let down my defenses, but I had determined to never give myself to Dony or anyone again.

My walls were still intact.

Mother shot me one of those "come-on-now-you-can-do-better-than-that" looks. I managed to lean into the car and give him an arm's length hug, mumbling, "I really hope you get your life together, Dony..."

It always made him mad when I called him "Dony" instead of "sweetheart," "honey," or some other term of endearment.

It served him right.

Pure or Polluted?

My dad returned home from Atlanta and simply stated, "Well, I got him there." After that, he was oddly quiet about it all.

It was a week of silence.

Dony was prohibited from making any phone calls. Even though I didn't want to talk with him, I couldn't help jumping every time the phone rang.

How was he doing? Who was he scamming this time? Would anyone be able to pull him through his living hell?

My questions were answered when Dr. David Johnson called from the treatment center.

"Mrs. McGuire, we want you to know that your husband is doing unusually well. As a matter of fact, we can't quite understand why he hasn't suffered any negative withdrawal symptoms."

No way! I want him to have cold chills, hallucinations, stomachaches, the bends, and bow before the porcelain throne seven times a day!

"Really..."

"Yes. Actually, he spends most of his time helping other patients. He's prayed a couple of men through some long rough nights. Our nursing staff is quite appreciative of his help ..."

Yeah, right. He's probably trying to sneak drugs while you're not looking.

"When Mr. McGuire was admitted, he claimed to be less than 24 hours sober. While we're not disputing him, our tests reveal no trace of foreign chemicals in his blood or urine."

That conniver!

"I'm sorry, doctor, but either your equipment is faulty or he's conned somebody into peeing in a cup for him," I snapped. "Maybe he switched the blood samples, 'cause Dony McGuire's test results should be 100 proof!"

"Well, ma'am, that's what we need to find out. A team of European doctors is here at the Center researching the long-term effects of addiction on the human body. Your husband mystifies them. They would like your permission to run special bone marrow tests on him."

"What does that mean?"

"Bone marrow tests along with other procedures will detect any foreign chemicals in the body during the previous 11 months. We need to test Mr. McGuire to determine the full extent of his addiction and to ensure he hasn't sabotaged the blood and urine samples."

"Look, Doc, I'm sure Dony talked you into phoning me, but I couldn't care less what happens to him."

The curtness in my voice surprised both of us.

"I'm in the process of filing for divorce so help yourself," I clipped sharply. "You can cut off his other leg for all I care!"

I slammed the phone, half-hating myself for being so harsh, especially to a kind doctor who was only trying to help us. But I didn't want his help! I just wanted Dony McGuire out of my life, once and for all.

Here Come the Good Guys

Pastor Duane Swilley of Chapel Hill Harvester Church in Atlanta committed himself to visiting Dony every day at the treatment center. I couldn't understand why Duane extended himself. We had met him and senior pastor, Bishop Earl Paulk, only once before. They barely knew us. It seemed peculiar to me that they would want to reach out to Dony.

When Duane phoned to give me an unsolicited update on Dony's progress, he invited me to fly to Atlanta and perform a short concert at their church on a Sunday evening. His adorable wife, Sunny, was on the line adding her warm welcome sprinkled with southern humor. I heard myself laugh for the first time in weeks.

I don't know why...but I agreed to a concert date two weeks later.

The next day, Dony got permission to phone me about an upcoming conference the treatment center was hosting. The conference, ironically scheduled for the Monday and Tuesday after my Chapel Hill concert, was designed to help families of addicts deal with their dysfunctional lives.

"Reba, I'm just beginning to understand the hell I've put you through," Dony admitted meekly. "You don't even have to see me if you don't want to. The workshops are really just for you. They say this is a good time for you to tell your side of the story."

The chance to set the record straight.

I don't know why...but that appealed to me.

Two weeks later, Duane and Sunny picked me up at the airport.

"The church has reserved a beautiful hotel suite for you," Sunny chirped. "But we would be honored for you to stay in our home instead. You'd have your own bed and bathroom and we promise not to bother you. Besides, I'm a great cook!"

I don't know why I said yes...but that appealed to me.

God was slowly rebuilding my ability to trust again. He used precious people like Duane and Sunny, Bishop Earl and Norma Paulk, Pastors Don and Clariece Paulk, and others to pour in the oil and wine.

The concert at Chapel Hill went well. The pastors and congregation readily accepted me in spite of me. I now understand it was because they have been taught that some special guests come to minister *to* them while others—like me—come to be ministered to *by* them.

・◡ ◡・

*D*ony must have been watching for me. Monday morning, I entered the complex doors and he was waiting right there to welcome me. He had already gained ten much needed pounds. He was more muscular from the compulsory physical workouts. His face glowed with renewed health. He looked great.

Darn!

"I just came to tell you I'm glad you're here, Reba. It means a lot to me," he hugged carefully. "At the end of your afternoon session, I'll be in the courtyard. I could show you around a little bit if you'd like...and maybe you could have supper with me."

There was a calmness, genuineness, and gentleness in his demeanor that rattled me to the core.

"I can't make any promises," I coughed nervously. "I'm just taking this one step at a time."

"Okay, take all the time you need," he assured. "I'll be waiting in the courtyard no matter what you decide."

I don't know why...but I believed him.

I really liked the staff at the treatment center, especially Dr. Elizabeth Payton. Her father was an alcoholic and she had been sexually abused as a child. She had followed in her father's footsteps and had become an alcoholic as a teenager.

I had never seen a doctor step outside the exalted "professional mode" and become so transparent and vulnerable. She disarmed me and the other families with her honesty and humor. She helped us laugh again. Dr. Payton helped me realize I wasn't alone. All those years, I had felt so isolated, as though I was the only one struggling with an addicted spouse. She told stories of people just like me who had learned there is life after addiction.

This was also the first time I had heard people talk so openly about sexual abuse.

Father Antonio, a Spirit-filled Catholic priest, conveyed his story of alcoholism and the resulting shame. He wept freely as he shared his saga: how he had finally hit bottom and had come to know that the "Higher Power" he sermonized and homilized was really real.

Later that afternoon, the staff asked probing questions and those family members who were brave enough—or angry enough—responded. An unusual camaraderie was forged between the families. I sympathized with them. I hurt with them. I screamed with them.

Peripheral Pain

The wife of a drug-addicted surgeon particularly intrigued me. They were from "old money" and owned three successful hospitals. The surgeon loved getting high...in more ways than one. On three separate occasions, he crashed small airplanes while flying under the influence, miraculously escaping death each time. The family could no longer cover for him and he lost his medical license. The courts ordered him into a treatment center.

At the end of the second session, one of the questions seemingly pushed the wrong button in the wealthy physician's wife. This classic beauty draped in sables and dripping with diamonds, spewed foul venom, reducing herself to common white trash. The more she regurgitated and profaned, the older and uglier she appeared.

Hell hath no fury like a woman scorned.

Finally, she lost control, raging, "I hate him for what he's done to me and my children! I can never...*never*...forgive him!!"

God, I don't want to end up like her! Please help me!

I AM. If you really don't want to be like her—you must learn to forgive.

When she stormed out, we just sat there stunned and horrified. The atmosphere gashed, reeking of bitterness, violation, and malignant rage.

Hurting people hurt people.

Dr. Payton broke the awkward silence. "You may not understand it now, but this is all a part of the healing process."

Sometimes healing hurts like hell.

If you don't believe it—just ask Jesus.

The Divine Contradiction

*F*orgiving others is such a huge issue.

I am overwhelmed by the sheer volumes of brilliantly written information and revelation on this vital subject of forgiveness. Excellent books on *how to* and *how not to...when to* and *when not to...why to* and *why not to...who should* and *who shouldn't...what happens if you do* and *what happens if you don't ...*

I want to focus attention on Jesus, our perfect example of forgiveness.

Every human being He was close to during His earthly walk rejected, abandoned, betrayed, denied, criticized, misunderstood, became offended, or tried to manipulate Him. Add the weight of carrying the sins of the whole world and you've got more than an opportunity for Jesus to harbor a root of bitterness. But He knew the quote He would drop into Francis Frangipane's spirit two thousand years later.

Bitterness is unfulfilled revenge.[2]

I picture Jesus hanging on Golgatha's cross, reliving blurred images of His last week.

"Passion Week"
Rejected for Messiah mission
Betrayed by handpicked treasurer
yAbandoned by ministr staff

Follow the Yellow Brick Road

Falsely accused
by the very ones He came to save
Repeatedly denied
by water-walking partner
Illegally arrested and tried
Exchanged for a seditious murderer
Condemned to a criminal's cross
Stripped naked
Beaten beyond recognition
Paraded twice
before palm-waving "Hosanna!" masses
twisted into
fist-raising "Crucify Him!" mobs

Forsaken by His Father

The greatest Giver of all time
suspended between two thieves
Strength nailed between weakness
Right in the midst of wrong
Innocence flanked by guilt
Light defied by darkness
Forgiveness taunted by bitterness

Love skewered by hate
Perfection embraced corruption
Eternity yielded to the hands of time
Life surrendered to ephemeral death

Resurrection[3]

In John 14:12, Jesus commissioned His followers to accomplish greater works than He did. Let's start with doing what He did: *forgive*.

190

All the while Jesus agonized on Calvary, He preached forgiveness...*from a cross.* He has given us the power to hang on our cross—whatever it may be—and still maintain focus.

As soldiers are driving jagged spikes into our flesh—we can still bestow clemency. "Father, forgive them; for they know not what they do."

As we are dying—we can still speak life. "Today you will be with Me in paradise."

As we are being separated from everyone we love—we can still minister adoption. "Woman, behold your son!...[Son], behold your mother!"

As we are being poured out for others—we can still crave the Living Water. "I am thirsty."

As we are feeling God-forsaken—we can still exude trust. "Father, 'into Your hands I commit My spirit.'"

As we are going through unimaginable changes—we can still declare unchangeable truth. "It is finished!"[4]

Snip, Snip Here—Clip, Clip There

God sent "wrecking and rebuilding crews" to dismantle the dysfunctional, crooked path my life had taken. I ran headlong into engineering experts who reconstructed a "highway of whole-y-ness."

Among many others in God's construction crew, Bishop Luther Blackwell was totally unaware of my devastated life when he spoke a prophetic word that triggered an immediate paradigm shift in me.

"I see a huge, dark, ominous cloud surrounding you. It has immobilized and almost suffocated the life out of you. But look up! What you perceived as a cloud of the enemy...God says, *'This night I am transforming your storm cloud into a rain cloud. The tears you shed have not gone unnoticed. I have kept them in a vial before My throne.*

Now I begin the process of pouring them out on you as showers of blessing. You will become like a well-watered garden...'"

———————— ·◡ ◠· ————————

GOLDEN STEPPING STONE
To forgive is divine.

———————— ·◡ ◠· ————————

Pam Rice is another one of God's glorified living stone rebuilders. A degreed counselor in Southern California, Pam packs a powerful one-two punch. She is a highly respected, educated, and experienced professional; and she operates in the gifts of the Spirit (words of wisdom, knowledge, discerning of spirits) with anointing, sensitivity, and solid biblical principles. She is also my friend.

God used Pam's skill at this critical point in my life to help free me from years of unresolved anger; secret shame; brokenness; bitterness and unforgivingness.[5]

I phoned her one night from Atlanta and asked point-blank, "If you had a husband who'd done all the things to you that Dony's done to me, what would you do?"

Without hesitation, Pam answered, "I would love myself enough to forgive him."

"Tell me why."

"Holding grudges and keeping scorecards is damaging and self-destructive. I wouldn't want to reap the consequences of all that bitterness. *I wouldn't want to hurt myself*. Besides, there's nothing more unattractive than a bitter old prune-of-a-woman who only talks about her pain and misery. I've learned to like myself too much to do that to me."

"But I don't know if I can forgive him."

"Aren't you tired of carrying Dony around on your back?"

"Of course."

"Why don't you just give him to Jesus? Jesus is all for giving, not for taking...*for-giving*...for giving those who have hurt us back to Him. Reba, you can trust Him to deal with Dony. To heal him..."

If you forgive someone's sins, they're gone for good. If you don't forgive sins, what are you going to do with them? (John 20:23 TM)

Person-by-person, layer-by-layer, hurt-by-hurt, offense-by-offense...God was teaching me how to forgive.

Dony.

My childhood abuser.

My first husband.

Myself.

It wasn't easy, but He responded to my desperation and obedience.

If you will only let Me help you, if you will only obey, then I will make you rich! (Isaiah 1:19 TLB)

If you are willing and obedient, you will eat the best from the land (Isaiah 1:19 NIV).

Forgiveness is a wonderful yet scary thing.

I felt like an airline baggage handler...losing tons of luggage I had carried around for years. I had become very familiar with hauling all that weight disguised as exclusive Louis Vuitton.

Sometimes I would surrender a heavy bag just to find myself scouring through the lost luggage department. But once I began to experience the joy of traveling light, I memorized the phone number of Goodwill.

People of good will are always willing to take old suitcases off your hands.

In my quest for understanding, I stumbled across these significant observations about forgiveness in' the *International Standard Bible Encyclopedia*.[6]

> "Christ taught that forgiveness is a duty. **No limit can be set to the extent of forgiveness (Luke 17:4) and it must be granted without reserve.** Jesus will not admit that there is any wrong so gross nor so often repeated that it is beyond forgiveness. **To Him an unforgiving spirit is one of the most heinous of sins** (Bruce, Parabolic Teaching, 376ff). This is the offense which God will not forgive (Matthew 18:34, 35). It is the very essence of the unpardonable sin (Mark 3:22-30).
>
> "It was the one blemish of the elder son which marred an otherwise irreproachable life (Luke 15:28-30).
>
> "This natural, pagan spirit of implacability Jesus sought to displace by a generous, forgiving spirit. It is so far the essence of His teaching that in popular language 'a Christian spirit' is not inappropriately understood to be synonymous with a forgiving disposition. His answer to Peter that one should forgive not merely seven times in a day, but seventy times seven (Matthew 18:21, 22), shows that **He thought of no limit to one's forgiveness**...'if ye forgive not every one his

Him, and stay close to Him. He is your life, and He will let you live many years in the land (Deuteronomy 30:19b-20 NCV).

If you want to be forgiven by God, you must forgive others.

In prayer there is a connection between what God does and what you do. You can't get forgiveness from God, for instance, without also forgiving others. If you refuse to do your part, you cut yourself off from God's part (Matthew 6:14-15 TM).

A pastor told me about Sister Roberta, an elderly woman in his church who had died recently. A few weeks after the funeral, he was missing this saint who was like a second mother to him.

"Father, could you let me see Sister Roberta around Your throne?" he prayed earnestly. "I'd just love to visualize her glowing countenance."

She isn't here.

"What do You mean? If there ever was a saint, Sister Roberta was it! She never missed a service. She was a faithful tither...mighty prayer warrior," the pastor defended. "She was the backbone of our church! There must be some mistake."

As a young woman, she married a man who abused and abandoned her. She never forgave him...so I couldn't forgive her.

The pastor made inquiries with her family and discovered the hidden truth.

Hearing that story was a major wake-up call for me.

God isn't obligated to forgive me or even hear me if I don't forgive my trespassers. I desperately needed God's forgiveness, so I had to forgive Dony, myself, and anyone else who had wronged me.

Not even Dony McGuire was worth my burning in hell.

> *If you forgive people their trespasses [their reckless and willful sins, leaving them, letting them go, and giving up resentment], your heavenly Father will also forgive you. But if you do not forgive others their trespasses [their reckless and willful sins, leaving them, letting them go, and giving up resentment], neither will your Father forgive you your trespasses* (Matthew 6:14-15).

----------·༈ ༈·----------

GOLDEN STEPPING STONE
Forgive.
No one is worth your burning in hell.

----------·༈ ༈·----------

You can forgive others. When you try to forgive in your own strength, you will fail. *"I can do all things through Christ." Christ* isn't Jesus' last name. *Christ* literally means "the Anointed One and His anointing."

Many times Holy Spirit is trying to help you by releasing the anointing to forgive—a supernatural ability and enabling. Anytime you relinquish pride and by faith receive His yoke-destroying anointing, you can forgive.

> *I have strength for all things in Christ Who empowers me [I am ready for anything and equal to anything through Him Who infuses inner strength into*

me; I am self-sufficient in Christ's sufficiency]
(Philippians 4:13).

I was getting so desperate to be free from unforgive-ness that if some preacher had told me to go dip in the River Jordan seven times like Naaman, I probably would have done it!

Don't allow pride to keep you from running to the River. When Holy Spirit woos, yield.

Remember: you're not free until you *know* you're free.

Don't go back to the trap. To stay free, get rid of the scorecards. Burn them! If you know where you've hidden them, you haven't let them go. You're still imprisoned.

"Holy Spirit, help!" are three of the most powerful words you'll ever pray.

> *In [this] freedom Christ has made us free [and com-pletely liberated us]; stand fast then, and do not be hampered and held ensnared and submit again to a yoke of slavery [which you have once put off]* (Gala-tians 5:1).

Pray for those you forgive. It is difficult to stay mad at somebody you consistently pray for—not against.

Do yourself a favor.

Pray for your enemies. Bless them! Forgive them! Practice forgiving-ness.

> *[...make it a practice to] love your enemies, treat well, (do good to, act nobly toward) those who detest you and pursue you with hatred. Invoke blessings upon and pray for the happiness of those who curse you, implore God's blessing (favor) upon those who abuse you [who revile, reproach, disparage, and highhandedly misuse you]* (Luke 6:27b-28).

Endnotes

1. Thank you, Billye Brim.

2. Francis Frangipane, *The Three Battlegrounds* (Cedar Rapids, IA: Advancing Church Publishing, 1989), page number unknown.

3. "Passion Week" by Reba Rambo-McGuire and Judy A. Gossett. 2001 Rambo-McGuire Publishing. Used by permission.

4. Luke 23:34 KJV; Luke 23:43b NIV; John 19:27 NKJV; John 19:28b NIV; Luke 23:46b NKJV; Psalm 31:5; John 19:30b NIV.

5. Many computer spell check programs include the term "forgivingness" rather than "forgiveness." This implies an active—not passive—tense. Forgiving-ness. God intends for us to stay in an active, ongoing, ever-extending state of forgivingness.

6. *International Standard Bible Encyclopedia.* Electronic text and markup. Used by permission. Copyright 1998 by Epiphany Software.

"A Perfect Heart"

Morning sun
Light of creation
grassy fields
a velvet floor
silver clouds
a shimmering curtain
He's designed a perfect world

I'm amazed at His talents
stand in awe of One so great
Now my soul begins to sing out
to the Source
from which it came

Bless the Lord
who reigns in beauty
Bless the Lord
who reigns with wisdom
and with power
Bless the Lord
who reigns my life
with so much love
He can make a perfect heart[1]

Chapter 17

IF I ONLY HAD A BRAIN

What is it about a scarecrow who gets a new brain?

He will study unashamedly—taking the risk of the fire of God burning old hay and stubble—because he actually perceives the profound revelation: the same One' who conferred his new mind also possesses an endless supply of Truth.

Wisdom. God-knowledge. Understanding.

Good report. Purity. Virtue.

Honor. Praiseworthiness.

The mind of Christ.

The covenant of Peace. Nothing missing. Nothing broken.

You'll do best by filling your minds and meditating on things true, noble, reputable, authentic, compelling, gracious—the best, not the worst; the beautiful, not the ugly; things to praise, not things to curse. Put into practice what you learned from me, what you heard and saw and realized. Do that, and God, who makes everything work together, will work you into His most excellent harmonies (Philippians 4:8-9 TM).

The top of Dony's mahogany desk was still a mess, only this time it was covered with five different translations of the Bible, a couple of concordances, a half-filled notebook and stacks of teaching tapes. Foraging through the top drawer in search of a yellow highlighter, his eye caught the glint of a shiny razor blade he had once used to cut cocaine during his drug-dealing days.

How did I miss this one?

Returning home from the treatment center two weeks earlier, his first order of business was getting rid of all his drug paraphernalia and booze. What a project! One sweep of the house, garage, cars, shrubs, commode tanks, and deep freeze coughed up 18 bottles of vodka and thousands of dollars in illegal drugs.

He was amazed and eternally grateful for the Lord's love and intervention.

God, I want to thank You for delivering me...for being so good to me...for helping me understand Your Word and reprogramming this fried-out brain of mine. I just can't seem to get enough of You!

Dony was now feeding his new addictions. Craving for God. Intoxication with the Spirit. Hunger for the Word. Passion for Worship. With a renewed, sober mind, he finally understood why they call Yahweh "the Most High." No drug rush ever came close to the pure joy and sheer euphoria he had found in Jesus.

The phone ringing interrupted his moment with the Lord. Dony wiped his eyes and answered, "Hello?"

"Dony, this is Bishop Earl Paulk from Atlanta."

"It's sure good to hear from you, Bishop! I was just thinking about you a little while ago!"

"Son, I was praying for you and Reba this morning...and God said to send you airline tickets to come to Atlanta. Our church is supposed to be a hospital for you two...we're going to help restore you."

"Wow, that sounds good, Bishop, but you need to know that Reba isn't here...she's living with her parents...and doesn't want anything to do with me. I can't imagine her being willing to go to Atlanta or anywhere with me right now."

"That's okay, son. If you'll just come to Atlanta, we'll let God deal with Reba."

The Joke Was on Me

*B*ishop Paulk immediately phoned me.

"Reba darlin', I was praying for you and Dony this morning...and God said to send you airline tickets to come to Atlanta. Our church is supposed to be a hospital for you two...we're going to help restore you."

"Well, Bishop...Dony and I aren't together. I'm just trying to get on with my life. Besides, I can't imagine Dony allowing any church to restore him."

"That's okay, darlin'. If you'll just come to Atlanta, we'll let God deal with Dony."

*C*huckling to himself, Bishop promptly phoned the travel agent, booked the flight, specified adjoining seats and couriered tickets to each of us.

Imagine my astonishment when I boarded the Delta Airlines red-eye in Los Angeles and "guess who?" was sitting in the next seat. The startled expression on Dony's face conveyed he hadn't expected to see me either.

I moved three rows back.

Confrontation/Negotiation

*T*wo cars picked us up at the Atlanta Airport. Same hotel. Different floors. Separate rooms.

For the next two weeks, Dony was Bishop Paulk's shadow. Breakfast-lunch-and-dinner, weddings, funerals, church services, hospital visits, whatever. This great man of God took Dony under his wings. Why? Bishop understood the anointing is as much *caught* as taught.

My mornings were spent with Pastor Lynn Mayes, Chapel Hill's gifted Spirit-led counselor. Graciously walking me through the multi-layered issues of my life, Pastor Lynn let me open up, vent, cry, yell at her, and even use language that should have melted her clerical collar.

I don't think I rattled her cage once.

One afternoon, I reluctantly agreed that Dony and I would meet together with Bishop and various staff pastors. Glaring at Dony across the foreboding conference table, my body language said it all.

Arms folded tightly.

Chin set.

My heart smoldering with anger, bitterness, and distrust.

I don't even like you anymore!

Ironically, Dony was thinking the very same about me.

"I want you both to know...I'm not trying to get the two of you back together again," Bishop reassured. (That was the only lie I've ever heard the Bishop tell.)

"Our purpose is to get each of you healed. To accomplish that, we're going to help you face some painful issues."

At the end of those two weeks, I was emotionally wrung out like a dishrag. Spiritually, I was being refreshed and renewed by attending church almost every day; being embraced by the unconditional love of the open-hearted people at Chapel Hill; listening to Bishop's brilliant sermons; worshiping in the rich presence of God; experiencing Pastor Duane's energized Monday night youth explosion called *Alpha*...and somebody praying with me every 47 minutes.

Duane's wife, Sunny, certainly lives up to her name. She was so good for me. My "pity parties" were completely ruined by her encouragement, contagious effervescence, and zest for life.

I was changing in spite of myself. Changing from the inside out.

Dony and I returned to L.A. and our separate lives only to find ourselves back in Atlanta a couple of weeks later.

"Reba, do you trust Dony?" Bishop probed.

"No, sir."

"Do you trust me?"

"Yes, sir."

"I'm going to make you this promise. You will never have to deal with Dony's addiction again."

"What do you mean? Are you guaranteeing he'll never have a problem with drugs or alcohol?"

"No, I'm promising that *you* will never have to deal with it again."

Blue x-ray eyes blazing, Bishop turned to Dony. "Son, if you ever mess up again, you're going to have to deal with *me*. You've got to be accountable to someone and I don't see anyone else willing to go to bat for you...but I am willing to cover you. Understand this: the only way I will counsel this little lady to go back into relationship with you...is for you to promise me that if you even *think* about stumbling...you will call me immediately."

A lump in his throat, Dony merely shook his head yes.

"Dony, I am going to lift you up to my level of trust in you. I choose to believe the best of you." Bishop turned to face me. "Reba, the only way I'll counsel Dony to get back with you is for you to make me the same promise."

I hesitated a moment and then agreed.

Bishop instructed us to take a couple of days to prepare individual lists of our goals and desires for how we could have a healthy marriage.

We compared notes and Bishop helped draw up a Covenant Agreement including ongoing counseling. Attending church together. Tithing. Getting our finances in order. Praying and studying the Word. Submitting to spiritual authority. Communicating honestly. Forgiving one another. Refusing to live in the past. Having weekly date nights. Attending 12-step meetings. Flying to Atlanta at least one Sunday a month.

I don't know whose hand was shaking the most when we finally signed our covenant pledge.

———— ·⤳ ⤲· ————

GOLDEN STEPPING STONE
Covenant agreements are powerful!
They help clarify boundaries.

———— ·⤳ ⤲· ————

Nearly one thousand young people jammed the auditorium for Monday night *Alpha*. Sunny and I were packed like sardines in the gyrating crowd. From the stage, the rock 'n roll praise band blared, smoke machines fogged, lights throbbed, pyrotechnics exploded. I'd never been in a church service like that before. Concerts, yes. But not church.

Out of the corner of my eye, I noticed Dony walk in with the Bishop.

After signing our covenant pledge, I was gradually growing more comfortable with the idea of being around him, but I still harbored reservations.

"I want you to share your testimony tonight, Dony," Bishop urged. "These kids need to hear what God has done for you."

"Me? Here? Tonight?" Dony back-pedaled. "Don't you think I need at least a year's sobriety? Besides, all these kids are saved."

"That's what you think. We've got all kinds of young people who only come to hear the music and have fun. Don't panic. You'll do fine."

Kids respectfully cleared a path for Bishop as he shepherded a very reluctant Dony to the platform.

"I never talk on stage! I just play the piano and sing," Dony protested. "What am I supposed to say? It's too soon."

Bishop leaned closer to Dony's ear. "Don't put a time frame on your deliverance. That's not important. Just tell them what happened the night Jesus walked into your room."

Handing a microphone to Dony, Bishop waved him onto the stage and into the spotlight. Dony just stood there. Speechless. Sweating. Terrified.

The crowd grew awkwardly silent, waiting for something. Anything.

Pastor Duane rescued him by putting an arm around his shoulder, announcing, "I want you to welcome Grammy-award winner...and my friend, Dony McGuire!"

The crowd applauded politely and Dony found his voice. "I was a big-time alcoholic and a drug addict...I messed around on my wife..." he began.

Thirty minutes later, more than two hundred young people sobbed at the foot of the stage. Dony and Duane jumped down and began moving among them.

Praying. Weeping.

Loving. Touching.

Embracing. Pointing the way to Jesus.

Spontaneously, kids pushed through the crowd and threw stuff into offering baskets on the stage. All kinds of drugs. Nickel bags of marijuana. Mini-bottles of liquor. Packs of cigarettes. Condoms. Birth control pills. Pornographic magazines. Weapons. Filling basket after basket.

Talk about an offering! If the Vice Squad had showed up, we would have been busted for sure.

By this time, I was a certifiable mess. This was a four-hanky event and true to form...I didn't even have a wadded up *Kleenex*. I was mesmerized when Dony leapt onto the stage, sat down behind the keyboard and began "It's My Desire,"[1] a song he'd made famous years before. Only this time, he knew what he was singing about.

"It's my desire to live for Jesus
It's my desire to be like Him
Though often I fail and bring Him much shame
It's my desire to live for Him."

Remember the night Dony was lying on your bed covered with Bibles and I asked you to see a potential Christ in him?

Yes, Sir.

What do you see now?

Dony wept Jesus' tears. He sang Jesus' heart. He embraced Jesus' passion. I never knew Jesus played piano, but that night He did.

*"If you could see where Jesus brought me from
To where I am today
Then you would know the reason why I love Him so
Now you can take the world's wealth and riches
I don't need earth's fame
It's my desire to live for Him."*

By James Pearse Reid

**Get a good look, Reebs. I AM up to something wonderful...
and this is only the beginning. Trust what I AM doing in him.**

Someone turned on a single spotlight and triggered the fog machine. Dony was enveloped in a dense, luminous mist. Holy Spirit nudged my memory of Luther Blackwell's prophetic word.

"What you perceived as a cloud of the enemy...God says 'This night, I AM transforming your storm cloud into a rain cloud...'"

I was inexplicably drawn to the edge of the stage where man-made fog morphed into supernatural billows of brooding, hovering, swirling Glory.

"'...The tears you shed have not gone unnoticed. I have kept them in a vial before My throne. Now I begin the process of pouring them out on you as showers of blessing.'"

"Holy Inundation" *a Flood — a condition of Superabundance*

*An innumerable Host of angels
uncorked, upturned, unleashed
the Heaven-sized vial of tears
Love's tidal wave Baptism
cast off, cast down, cast out
the hell-sized imps of Fear*

*Stripping invisible layers
of my familiar armor
Willfulness, Rights, Anger, Pride
Blame, Suspicion, Rejection, Lies*

211

Follow the Yellow Brick Road

Victim robes discarded
Vulnerable, unashamed
Trembling, testing, touching, trusting
Turning, tumbling, transforming, triumphing

Immanuel Fountainhead pierced
Sea of Red beckoned

I played in the Puddle
I danced in the Downpour
I swam in the Surge
I died in the Deep

I surrendered to the Holy Flood
as the dragon fangs
melted into nothingness

Holy Whirlwind untwisted Hopelessness
uncurling never-ending Rainbow of Promise[2]

And [I] *came to* [myself] (Luke 15:17a KJV).

＊ ＊ ＊

*O*f all acts, is not, for man, repentance the most Divine?

＊ ＊ ＊

*T*he following night—four and one half months after Dad had carried me out of my house—Dony carried me back across the same threshold.
And we knew each other in the biblical sense.

＊ ＊ ＊

*P*aradise lasted only a couple of days.

Drug dealers and junkies usually aren't very good with money. Dony had been no exception. It was a harsh slap in the face when he finally confessed our financial disaster: we were $250,000 in debt.

Bill collectors and creditors were phoning around the clock, relentlessly hounding us for overdue payments. An attorney friend gave us some free advice. "You'll never dig your way out of this mess. File bankruptcy."

Everything in me wanted to return to the old, familiar patterns of blame and shame. After I screamed and yelled, Dony suggested we fast and pray for an answer from the Lord.

We did.

Everywhere we went, every time we turned on Christian TV or listened to a new teaching tape, somebody was talking about giving. Sowing seeds for a miracle. Testifying about unusual financial breakthroughs.

When we read the Bible together, verses about money and sowing seeds leapt off the pages.

Dony and I started by repenting for mishandling funds. For being reckless with our money. Then we gave away clothes from our closets, food from our cupboards, coins from our piggy bank and anything else that wasn't nailed to the floor.

We considered everything as seed Jesus could use to bless others and to help turn around our mess.

———— ·◟ ◞· ————

GOLDEN STEPPING STONE

Give your way out of debt.

———— ·◟ ◞· ————

*L*iving on a monthly retainer from our record-ing and song publishing royalties, we decided to cooperate when the Lord began unfolding a radical plan.

Sow all your personal income from royalties. Watch Me bless the ministry and provide for your needs.

Two days later when the royalty check came in, we tithed and then sowed the rest.

I was amazed at the way God was changing Dony's thinking. Renewing his mind with divine Wisdom.

He would think of things he'd never thunk before!

Don't let pride keep you from being honest with your creditors. Truth sets you free.

Dony promptly phoned or wrote letters to each of our creditors. He freely admitted to having been a drug dealer and an alcoholic. He boldly explained how Jesus had set him free. He let them know our lawyer had recommended filing bankruptcy but we didn't feel right about that. Then he asked them to give us one year to pay back *all*—not just a portion—of our debt. Every creditor—without exception—agreed. That was a miracle in and of itself!

We kept our word and started paying our debts. Dony stayed in regular communication with creditors and told the-truth-the-whole-truth-and-nothing-but-the-truth-so-help-him-God. Money appeared from the strangest places. God was showing up and showing off.

Looking back at our financial records for that year, we can't explain how it happened: *within 12 months, we were completely out of debt.*

You're out of the woods...you're out of the dark... you're out of the night...

My God will liberally supply (fill to the full) your every need according to His riches in glory in Christ Jesus (Philippians 4:19).

214

When a man is trying to please God, God makes even his worst enemies to be at peace with him (Proverbs 16:7 TLB).

Our steps are made firm by the Lord, when He delights in our way; though we stumble, we shall not fall headlong, for the Lord holds us by the hand. I have been young, and now am old, yet I have not seen the righteous forsaken or their children begging bread. They are ever giving liberally and lending, and their children become a blessing (Psalm 37:23-26 NRSV).

Endnotes

1. "It's My Desire" by Jimmy Pearce. 1976 Crown Royal. Used by permission.

2. "Holy Inundation" by Reba Rambo-McGuire and Judy A. Gossett. 2001 Rambo-McGuire Publishing. Used by permission.

"Because of Whose I Am"

I'll never understand
why He saw a piece of clay and said,
"I want it, I'll use it"
The greatest mystery is that somehow in spite of me
He said, "I'm gonna love you"
He took me in His arms
said, "This child belongs to Me"
He placed me in His kingdom now I live like royalty
It's not because of what I am
Not because of what I've done
It's because of Whose I am

I'll never understand
while I was yet a slave
He said He'd buy me, He'd save me
He clothed Himself in flesh became the Final Sacrifice
so I could know redemption
He took the stripes upon His back so that I can walk in health
Then He broke the chains of death now I can live forevermore
It's not because of what I am
Not because of what I've done
It's because of Whose I am

My Father is Lord of everything from here, beyond forever
He's given me His name, said if I'd ask anything
He'd gladly give it
He put a robe upon my back, placed a ring upon my hand
said the riches of Heaven were all mine
It's not because of what I am, not because of what I've done
but because He first loved me, His grace has set me free
His blood is flowing through my veins
I'm adopted by the King
It's because of Whose I am[m]

Chapter 18

COURAGE OF A LION

What is it about a lion who gets new courage?

He will roar unashamedly—taking the risk of sounding ridiculous—because he actually perceives the profound revelation: the same One who conferred his boldness also possesses an endless supply of Weapons.

Sword of the Spirit. Shield of Faith. Belt of Truth.

Breastplate of Righteousness. Helmet of Salvation.

Boots of Peace. Constant Intercession.

Perfected Praise.

Shout of Victory.

The Faith of God.

The covenant of Peace. Nothing missing. Nothing broken.

It is true that I am an ordinary, weak human being,[1] but I don't use human plans and methods to win my battles. I use God's mighty weapons, not those made by men, to knock down the devil's strongholds. These weapons can break down every proud argument against God and every wall that can be built to keep men from finding Him. With these weapons I can capture rebels and bring them back to God and change them into men whose hearts' desire is obedience to Christ (2 Corinthians 10:3-5 TLB).

The wicked flee when no man pursues them, but the [uncompromisingly] righteous are bold as a lion (Proverbs 28:1).

Headache-from-hell pounds with relentless rhythm of a metronome ball bat.

Abdomen shudders from scalpeled hoof prints left by a thousand bucking broncos.

Nausea crawls up anesthesia-laced esophagus.

Veins sizzle as slow-dripping liquids ooze through a plastic umbilical cord.

Pupils contract under stabbing, merciless light.

My third corrective surgery nightmare. There's the good news and bad news.

First the good news: no hysterectomy.

The bad news? No babies.

Struggle for Survival

*N*othing smells quite like a hospital.

Colorful, designer-arranged bouquets of exotic, aromatic flowers barely masked the sterilized odor. Industrial strength cleansers thinly veiled the unmistakable stench of sickness and death.

At 12:15 a.m., visiting hours were long since over.

"It's been a mighty full day for everybody. Both of you need to get some rest." The veteran head nurse gently

shooed Dony away from my bed, her good-natured toler-
ance waning. Her voice was sweet as sun-ripened pineap-
ples from her native Jamaica.

"Your woman's tired out. Don't you worry, Mister.
Sophie's gonna take good care of her. Ain't gonna let noth-
in' bad happen on my shift..."

As the door closed behind Dony, she assessed me with
a long, practiced look. "Are you through bein' the Rock of
Gibraltar? Baby, you've gotta have somethin' for that
pain."

I nodded weakly, turning to face the window so she
wouldn't see the tear slip over the bridge of my nose and
fall like a thunderclap onto the pillow.

*How many more humiliating procedures? How many
more quick-spreading tumors? How many more experimental
drug treatments? How many more painful miscarriages? How
many more head-shaking doctors? How many more monthly
disappointments?*

Today was the final blow. The verdict was in. The
panel of specialists was unanimous. In spite of three corrective surgeries, I would never be able to carry a pregnancy to full term. I would never give birth and hold my
own babies in my arms.

•⁀ ⁀•

*I*nitially when I couldn't seem to get pregnant,
my doctor wasn't overly concerned. To placate
my anxiety, he loaded me up with books on conception,
gave me a basal thermometer and temperature charts.

I'll never forget storming into the recording studio
during a session Dony was producing.

"Come on, honey! It's time!" I announced breathlessly.

Dony grinned, patted my tummy and gave me one of those "here-we-go-again" looks. "Okay, guys...take a long lunch break."

The recording engineer and musicians snickered as I dragged my sheepish husband out the door.

The nearest hotel was one of those sleazy, rent-by-the-hour establishments with '70s red shag carpet on the walls and mirrors on the ceiling above the waterbed. We laughed ourselves silly.

By the time I'd had my third miscarriage, we weren't laughing anymore.

・ゝ ～・

*S*irens wailing in the distance announced the approach of a couple of ambulances, fire trucks or some emergency vehicle.

Must have been a bad accident. Come on, Reba. Snap out of it! You've got so many things to be thankful for.

Lying on the lumpy hospital bed, I forced myself to count my blessings.

Father, I thank You because I wasn't in that accident.

The hell of Dony's addiction is finally extinguished.

You are giving us a brand new marriage because the old one wasn't worth a hill of beans.

Our relationship with Dionne is starting to heal and flourish.

You've opened a whole new world of God-friendships for us.

We miraculously escaped bankruptcy.

We made it through an intense series of required study...we were officially ordained into the ministry.

Your fresh fountain of creativity has produced some divinely inspired songs.

Being thankful was helpful, but my heart was still heavy.

Father, what about Your promise? What about the vision?

The Vision

*D*ony and I had been married for three weeks. We had flown with our band into Dallas, Texas, for a big concert at Six Flags amusement park. The promoter had graciously lodged us in a beautiful suite at the Hyatt Regency. Dony was in the bathroom brushing his teeth as I sat at a desk in the parlor and carefully applied stage make-up.

Hope I can remember that new song arrangement tonight.

Concentrating on the lighted mirror, my periphery caught the image of a little boy toddling around the corner.

"There's a kid in here!" I yelped, rising to follow him.

"What did you say?" Toothpaste foaming around his mustached lips, Dony jerked the door open. "Who's here?"

"Honey, I just saw a little boy run around this corner. He's got to be here somewhere. Help me look for him."

"How in the world did a kid get in here?"

"I don't know. Maybe he's hiding somewhere. Check the closet."

We scoured the suite, searching under beds, in the closets, bathtub and armoire, between suitcases, behind curtains...but the little boy was nowhere to be found.

"Must have been your old friend Germs," Dony teased, returning to the bathroom to wipe off the dried toothpaste.

"No, I really did see someone. Maybe he just snuck out," I concluded. "His mother must be frantic."

221

I settled back in front of my make-up mirror.

Hmmm. That was bizarre.

Suddenly, there he was again. The same little boy...

"There he is!"

I was up like a flash and sprinted around the corner, only this time the bathroom door was wide open and Dony was standing there staring at me.

"Where did he go?" I shoved Dony into the sink, peering behind the shower curtain. "Didn't you see him?"

"Honey, there's nobody here." His brow creased with worry.

"But I *know* I saw him! A cute little boy...with curly hair. Wearing cut-offs and a t-shirt. He can't be more than two years old!"

"Baby, I've been standing here the whole time and nobody but you came around that corner." He drew me into his arms and lightly kissed my cheek. "I know you're tired, but we've got to leave for *Six Flags* in less than an hour."

Pulling myself away, I mumbled, "I'm not tired or crazy, Dony! I *know* what I saw..."

I trudged back to the parlor and plopped on the edge of the bed.

His name is Israel Anthem McGuire ... He will have the song of the true Israel in his heart ... His initials are I.A.M. He will be a son of God.

Epiphany

ather, what was that vision all about? Why would You show me that if You weren't going to give me a son?

Sophie returned to take my vital signs, injected the pain medication and sleeping aid into my IV bag and patted my shoulder. "Okay, Missy. You press the call button if you need anything."

Lord, You wouldn't tease me. I know You gave me that vision all those years ago for a reason.

The medications were taking effect and I slowly sank into drugged slumber.

•⁀ ‿•

*B*ack at our home, Dony threw himself across the antique four-poster bed. Exhausted, he closed his eyes and rubbed his throbbing temples. All he could see were the sad faces of the specialists and hear their gloomy voices.

"Even after surgery, Mrs. McGuire still has multiple complications...virtually impossible for her to bear children...she's been through so much, if you really want children, you should contact an adoption agency..."

Lord, I feel like such a failure. Reba and I can't even keep Your first commandment to be fruitful and multiply. Do You want us to adopt? We need a clear word from You, Father.

He clutched a down feather pillow to his chest and sobbed.

God, I'm a tither. You promised to rebuke the devourer for our sake...so what's the problem? Why can't Reba and I have children?

Because you believe the doctors more than Me.

Dony froze. Truth startled him into faith.

Remember...you are to call things that are not as though they were.

Dony jumped up, raced back to the hospital and awakened me with these words: "Honey, you're pregnant!"

I thought I was having a nightmare. He shook me by the shoulders and repeated, "Honey, I said you are pregnant!"

"Yeah, right," I drooled groggily. "You haven't been drinking again, have you?"

"No, I've never been more sober in my life. I just heard from God..."

He left the hospital, drove straight to Beverly Hills and spent the rest of the night in a vacant parking lot. Early the next morning when the doors opened to an exclusive Beverly Hills maternity shop, Dony was waiting. He purchased a gorgeous satin maternity dress and had it beautifully gift-wrapped.

Two days later I was released from the hospital. Dony carefully helped me into the car, placed a small pillow behind my back and securely fastened my seatbelt.

"Honey, I've got a surprise for you."

Reaching into the back seat, he pulled out the elaborate package. I opened the box, oohed appreciatively at the exquisite design and fingered the smooth, delicate fabric.

"Thank you, sweetheart. This is absolutely beautiful," I exclaimed, "but it looks too big."

"It's supposed to be big...it's a maternity dress!"

My countenance fell and I stared out the side window.

A maternity dress! Why in the world is he doing this? It's painful enough without another reminder ...

Dony was undaunted as he started the car and headed toward the freeway. He always whistles when he's having a good day.

"Did you miss your turn?" I questioned. "This isn't the way home."

"We're not going home yet. I have another surprise." Dony's blue-gray eyes were sparkling. He had set up an appointment with a photographer, hairstylist, and makeup artist for a photo shoot...to take a portrait of me in the maternity dress.

Ask me how thrilled I was. Not!

When we arrived at the studio, the professionals worked their magic, handling me with kid gloves. They followed Dony's instructions to the tee: he wanted a profile shot of me wearing the maternity dress with the car pillow plumped against my stomach, my hands cradling the bulky silhouette.

How embarrassing! How absurd can you get!

But when Dony explained his reasoning, a spark of faith ignited inside me too.

"Honey, you've got to understand. I want to picture you pregnant," Dony reassured me. "If I can see it—I can seize it."

If I can see it—I can seize it? Yes! If I can see it—I can seize it!

*...God who gives life to the dead and who **creates something out of nothing**. There was no hope that Abraham would have children. But Abraham believed God and continued hoping, and so he became the father of many nations (Romans 4:17b-18 NCV).*

———— ·⏘ ⏗· ————

GOLDEN STEPPING STONE
If you can see it—You can seize it!

———— ·⏘ ⏗· ————

Dony framed a pregnancy portrait for his desk and another one for his bedside nightstand. When people would see the desk photo and ask, "Is Reba pregnant?"...he would respond, "Isn't she?"

Every day Dony called me "pregnant." After awhile, I called me "pregnant" too.

Bethel Church in Riverside, California, pastored by our spiritual parents, Drs. Ron and Annie Halvorson, included me in their prayer chain for barren women. They also faxed Scripture verses on childbearing that Dony and I diligently spoke in anticipation of our miracle baby.

We asked the Lord to give us lots of seed. Seed to sow, not seed to eat.

Now He who supplies seed to the sower and bread for food will also supply and increase your store of seed and will enlarge the harvest of your righteousness. You will be made rich in every way so that you can be generous on every occasion (2 Corinthians 9:10-11 NIV).

God supernaturally sent us monies we gladly sowed for our expected harvest. We named each seed "miracle baby."

It was our great joy to furnish and decorate two couples' nurseries. We also paid the maternity hospital bill for a missionary couple home on furlough when their baby was born. In November of that year, we were challenged to sow our largest, most costly seed: donating nine thousand of our music cassettes for a Trinity Broadcasting Network telethon.[2]

That same week of Telethon, I conceived!

A difficult pregnancy, I battled morning sickness, gestational diabetes, bleeding, spotting, placenta previa, and other threatening symptoms of miscarriage. But this pregnancy was different because *we* were different. Dony and I were armed and dangerous...and more spiritually prepared for the enemy's attacks.

At 5½ months, we were filming in Miami, Florida, for TBN. Returning to the hotel around 1:00 a.m., I began hemorrhaging. The pain in my stomach was excruciating. Dony laid me on the bed, elevated my feet above my head on a mountain of pillows, stuffed towels around me, and started praying like a mad man.

One of the benefits of being in covenant relationships with great men and women of God is having the freedom to phone them at 2:00 in the morning. Dony called Bishop Paulk, quickly explained the crisis and held the phone to my ear as Bishop prayed a powerful prayer of faith. Within five minutes, all symptoms of miscarriage ceased.

As I slept soundly and peacefully for the next twelve hours, Dony phoned my physician and described the close call.

"She's obviously miscarried, Mr. McGuire," he stated flatly. "Since the bleeding has stopped, let her recoup for a couple of days...then bring her home for an ultrasound and probably a D&C."

Three days later, we went straight from the airport to the lab and my doctor ran some preliminary tests. He could detect no fetal heartbeat and quietly pulled Dony aside to explain his negative findings.

"You probably won't want to go in with her for the ultrasound," he cautioned.

"Of course I'm going in!" Dony replied. "I can't wait to see and hear my baby's strong heartbeat!"[3]

—— •◡ ◡• ——

GOLDEN STEPPING STONE
Sow a seed
in time of need.

—— •◡ ◡• ——

Two technicians, sobered by the doctor's gloomy prognosis, smeared my bulging belly with cold, clear gel and scanned the uterus. We watched intently as squishing, swirling, underwater sounds pulsated weird images on the monitor. Suddenly, we all heard and saw a tiny heart beating 90 miles an hour!

The doctor and technicians cheered loudly as my husband laughed, cried, and shouted praises all at the same time.

One of the technicians let slip, "She looks great!"

"What do you mean *she* looks great?" I inquired.

"I mean...the *baby* looks great," the embarrassed technician retracted.

"No, you said *she* looks great," I insisted.

The doctor addressed Dony, "If you'd like to know the gender, the baby is lying in the perfect position."

Dony looked at me, I bit my lower lip and nodded yes.

"*She* really does look great," the doctor confirmed. "You've got yourself one tough little girl!"

• ⌣ ⌣ •

Because of the vision and word from the Lord concerning Israel Anthem McGuire, we hadn't even considered our baby might be a girl. As we drove home, I was in shock and questioned my ability to accurately hear from God.

As soon as we walked in the door, I headed to the phone to call my parents with the news. Instead, the phone rang. Judy was on the other end.

"So how'd it go?" she asked with undisguised concern. "Everybody's been praying for you guys."

"The baby's fine," I burst into tears, "and *he's* a girl!"

Judy whooped, "That's great, Reeb!"

"But I was so sure I heard God tell me I was going to have a boy!" I wailed.

Judy chuckled, "Don't you get it, silly? If this baby's a girl, that just means you're going to have a boy next time!"

I hadn't even considered a *"next time"*...that would be too wonderful to be true!

⁓

Didn't I promise to do exceedingly, abundantly above all you could ask or think?

Yes, Father. I am overwhelmed with Your goodness to me.

If Israel had been born first, you would have relaxed your faith.

You know me too well.

⁓

"Reba, where'd you go? Are you still there?" she asked.

"Jude, do you realize this means we get to buy ruffles and ribbons...and sign up for ballet lessons...and have tea parties and play dress-up!" I exuded as the realization of this extravagant double portion sank in.

"Yes...and I'll teach her how to spell since you can't," Judy teased.

"I gotta call my mother and tell her to sew lots of pearls on the christening gown she's designing!" I raced. "Can you believe it, Jude? *I'm gonna have a baby girl!*"

Miracles Birthed

On August 12, 1986, Destiny Rambo McGuire made her debut before a roomful of cheering-weeping-deliriously-happy family and friends.

From her very first breath, I was a goner.

With her gentle sweetness, Destiny has filled a vacancy inside me that I didn't even know was there until she danced upon my heart.

She is my beautiful butterfly child.

⋅⤍ ⤏⋅

About a year later, my courageous, lion-hearted husband went before the Father. "God, if You did it once—You can do it again!"

On July 18, 1988, Israel Anthem McGuire wailed his first prophetic song before another roomful of cheering-weeping-deliriously-happy family and friends.

With his father's faith and his GrandDot's sensitivity to the Spirit, Israel has healed secret chambers inside me as he laughed across my heart.

Israel has his own invisible friends...only most of them are angels.

He is my little man of God.

⋅⤍ ⤏⋅

About a year later, when my crazy husband went before the Father to pray, "God, if You

230

did it twice—You can do it again!"...I interrupted and finished off his prayer, "but only if You make *Dony* give birth this time!"

Endnotes

1. Thank you, Danniebelle, for extracting the truth that God uses "Ordinary People" to accomplish extraordinary feats for His glory. Your songs are your legacy, living on in me and millions of other ordinary people.

2. Thank you, Paul and Jan Crouch and the TBN family for your love and prayers.

3. "Can two walk together, unless they are agreed?" Amos 3:3 NKJV. After a series of negative experiences, Dony and I changed doctors. We needed a physician who would support our stand of faith in God...not continuously speak words of death over our unborn child. The Lord directed us to a wonderful infertility specialist, Dr. Alton Hallum Jr. What a difference!

"The Only Snow"
(Dony's song)

Life was empty
I tried everything to fill it up
All the artificial thrills never were enough
Then You found me
and completely satisfied my life
and taught me soaring in Your arms
is the only way to fly

Now the only snow I care about
is on a frosty mountain peak
The only grass that turns me on is growing 'round my feet
The only smack I want to feel
is Reba's kiss upon my cheek
The greatest rush in all the world
is the love of You and me

Life is peaceful
There just ain't nobody else like You
All the temporary things don't calm me like You do
But if I'm tempted
the smile You give me
somehow makes me strong
and I've learned the purest form of Love
is all I need to get along

Now the only snow I care about
is on a frosty mountain peak
The only grass that turns me on is growing
'round my feet
The only smack I want to feel
is my children's kiss upon my cheek
The greatest rush in all the world
is the love of You and me

Reba's Epilogue

THERE'S NO PLACE LIKE HOME

~ 2001 ~

What is it about 3:00 in the morning?

I still watch them sleep.

She, with her long mane of chestnut hair cascading 'cross the teal pillow on her narrow top bunk of our touring coach. Taller than I, our Destiny, the beautiful ballerina with a size nine foot...or as we lovingly call her, "Dottie Rambo with legs."

He, two bunks beneath, cuddling a Beanie Baby, smelling of his father's cologne and rationed Peanut M&M's. Our resident rapper, practical joker, football fanatic, and bookworm who somehow taught himself to read at the age of four.

Across the aisle, Miss Tigger, our Jack Russell terrier, curls up at Cindy's knees. Rocked by the steady, thu-thumping heartbeat of the bus, Cindy doesn't budge as I gently remove her skewed, crackling headphones.

Thulthumping

*E*leven years ago, The Voice whispered a secret.

I AM sending you a treat.

I wondered if it would be a sparkling diamond ring, a shiny new car, or another material blessing. A few months later, Cindy Berry was hired as our children's governess and my personal assistant.

One night, I snuck into a jam-packed Sunday school room where Cindy's animated narration of Bible stories captivated Destiny, Israel, and a floor full of cross-legged, wide-eyed children. Cindy is the most gifted children's minister we know.

How do you like your treat?

Tears flowed freely. Father really had sent me a sparkling diamond in Miss Cindy...or as we lovingly call her, "The Ultimate Female." She has become my confidante, my right arm, and the glue holding our family together.

⌣ ⌣

*A*ll is well.

I confess: I'm a sleep watcher from way back.

How many nights since Dionne was three years old have I checked to see if she was okay?

Tonight, I carefully lift the curtain cocooning her top bunk. Our freckle-faced angel lies still as a stone in stark contrast to her childhood wild-as-a-miniature-tornado sleeping patterns. On this rare night together, I stare at the new wedding ring glistening on her slender finger as she dreams.

Seems like only yesterday she was clutching stinky green and yellow dandelions.

By the time Destiny was born, I was a seasoned pro at nighttime vigils. When Israel came along, I thought I'd get over it, but old habits die hard. I think my night watches began with making sure they were still breathing. How many times did I jostle them to reassure myself they were just asleep and not comatose?

Later my vigils became a quiet time when I could share my soul and whisper heart prayers.

So often I am better with a pen than speaking, but at 3:00 a.m., the fountain sometimes opens up and spills audible words. I find myself bragging on their accomplishments.

Dionne's amazing voice.

Destiny's remarkable stage persona.

Israel's passion for rap and dance.

But more than anything, I am thankful for their being three of the most delightful, likable, lovable children a mother could ever be blessed with. I marvel that God entrusted these treasures to Dony and me. Tonight, I quietly vow to tell them more often how proud I am to be part of three such generous spirits.

My late-night bed inspection ends with releasing them to the watchful care of their guardian angels.

I unlatch the sliding door and step into the darkened backroom glowing dimly from a tiny reading lamp. Dony lies spread-eagled on our bed covered with several Bibles, concordances, preaching notes, marking pens, and reading glasses.

The Word is getting into him, one way or another...only this time it's his own idea.

Chuckling to myself, I clear the bed and slip under the down comforter. Dony stirs and draws me into his safe, strong arms.

Father, I have to believe in miracles because I sleep with one. Thank You for not letting me kill him...look what I would have missed. You really have made new creatures out of us.

Our bus creaks and sways around another winding mountain road, ascending higher and higher. As dreams lure me deeper, a profound Truth skips through my consciousness.

The Road never ends. Our adventures are only beginning.

A Gentle Hand strokes my forehead. I stretch and purr expecting to see Dony's face silhouetted against the dim light. Instead...the familiar, luminous Glow.

I AM still watching you while you sleep.

I rub my frozen feet together, snuggle into Dony's warmth and sleepily smile heavenward.

There's no place like home...there's no place like home...there's no place like Home!

"The Road Home"

*W*here are you on your pilgrimage of life?

Have you been caught up in a whirlwind or two? Do you feel as though life has come crashing down? You may not know where on earth you are, but The Voice of Heaven woos, summoning you to a higher realm of destiny.

Perhaps you question, "Where do I start? How do I get to Jesus?" Follow me to the beginning of "the Romans Road" from *The Message*:

Step 1. Romans 3:23: "We've compiled this long and sorry record as sinners...and proved that we are utterly incapable of living the glorious lives God wills for us." Let's face it—we are all sinners in need of the Savior.

Step 2. Romans 6:23: "Work hard for sin your whole life and your pension is death. But God's gift is *real life*, eternal life, delivered by Jesus, our Master." Staying in the prison of sin will kill you, but Jesus holds the keys to set you free forever.

Step 3. Romans 5:8: "God put His love on the line for us by offering His Son in sacrificial death while we were of no use whatever to Him." We can never earn it or deserve it, but He loves us anyway.

Step 4. Romans 10:9-13: "This is the core of our preaching. Say the welcoming word to God—'Jesus is my Master'—embracing, body and soul, God's work of doing in us what He did in raising Jesus from the dead. That's it. You are not 'doing' anything; you're simply calling out to God, trusting Him to do it for you. That's salvation. With your whole being you embrace God setting things right, and then you say it, right out loud: 'God has set everything right between Him and me!' "

Pray these words from your heart: *"Jesus, I know I'm a sinner. I am so sorry for my sins. I believe You are the Son of God who died on the cross for me. I surrender my life to You now. Come into my heart. Give me a hunger for Your Word, a passion for Your presence and Your love for humanity. Show me Your path for my life. Thank You for setting everything right between You and me! In Jesus' Name, amen."*

If you believe what you just prayed—as a servant of the Most High God, by the authority of His Word and His Name—I declare: You are forgiven. You are pronounced "not guilty!" You have chosen the highway to Home. It's almost too good to be true...but it is true! As a matter of fact, angels are throwing a big party in Heaven right now. Why? Because once you were lost and now you're found.

What's the next step?

Tell somebody. Phone any of the following ministries and speak with a trusted prayer counselor. They will pray with you and send you free materials to help establish your commitment to Christ.

CBN—The 700 Club	800-759-0700
Life Today	800-947-5433
New Hope Counseling	714-539-4673
ORU Prayer Tower	918-495-7777
TBN	714-731-1000

Remember: you are not alone. You are now a born again child of God. You are a part of His family with millions of new brothers and sisters who are walking the same upward road Home.

I encourage you to get a Bible as soon as you can. This will tell you more about God's love and extraordinary plan for your life.

Pray. Talk to Him every day. Listen to The Voice as He whispers truth into your spirit.

Ask Him to lead you to a good church home with a loving, godly pastor.

Go back through this book, study the "Golden Stepping Stones" and apply them to your life.

Feel free to contact me at any time at P.O. Box 50508, Nashville, TN 37205 or www.rambomcguire.org. I would love to hear from you.

Be seeing you as we follow the Yellow Brick Road!

(And would you mind stuffing an extra *Kleenex* in your pocket for me?)

APPENDIX

～ *Crisis Hotlines* ～

All About Care   559-222-9471
(supports people infected and affected
by HIV/AIDS)
American Association of Christian Counselors 800-526-8673
(counseling referrals) www.aacc.net
Bethany Abortion Hotline   800-238-4269
(assisting with adoption, alternative to abortion)
www.bethany.org
CBN—The 700 Club   800-759-0700
(prayer counseling) www.cbn.org
Exodus Ministries   888-264-0877
(helping homosexuals and families)
www.exodusnorthamerica.org
Freedom Village   800-VICTORY
(help young people, drugs, prostitution, cults)
www.freedomvillageusa.com
Focus on the Family   800-232-6459
(counseling referrals) www.family.org

Hope House   207-777-3776
(supports sexually abused unwed mothers)
hopehouse@prodigy.net
Life Today   800-947-5433
(prayer counseling) www.lifetoday.org
Mercy Ministries of America   800-922-9131
(supports unwed mothers and adoption referrals)
www.mercyministries.org
Minirth-Meier New Life Clinics   800-639-5433
(help for psychological disorders and
compulsive behaviors) www.newlife.com
National AIDS Hotline   800-342-2437
(help for HIV/AIDS/STD)
New Hope Counseling   714-539-4673
(prayer counseling) www.newhopeonline.org
ORU Prayer Tower   918-495-7777
(prayer counseling) www.oru.edu
Pure Life Ministries   800-635-1866
(help for sexual addictions)
www.purelifeministries.org
Rapha   800-227-2657
(help for mental health and eating disorders)
www.raphacare.com
TBN   714-731-1000
(prayer counseling) www.tbn.org
Teen Challenge   800-814-5729
(help for addictions, life controlling problems)
Welcome Home Daughters   408-316-8681
(help for addictions and supports unwed
mothers, adoption referrals)

⌁ *Childbearing Scriptures* ⌁

Women will be saved through childbearing—if they continue in faith, love and holiness with propriety (1 Timothy 2:15 NIV).

No one shall suffer miscarriage or be barren in your land; I will fulfill the number of your days (Exodus 23:26 NKJV).

Blessed shall be the fruit of your body and the fruit of your ground and the fruit of your beasts, the increase of your cattle and the young of your flock (Deuteronomy 28:4).

Don't you see that children are God's best gift? the fruit of the womb His generous legacy? (Psalm 127:3 TM)

When I was still in my mother's womb He chose and called me out of sheer generosity! (Galatians 1:15 TM)

Before I formed you in the womb I knew you; before you were born I sanctified you; I ordained you a prophet to the nations (Jeremiah 1:5 NKJV).

He grants the barren woman a home, like a joyful mother of children. Praise the Lord! (Psalm 113:9 NKJV)

Then God blessed them, and God said to them, "Be fruitful and multiply; fill the earth and subdue it" (Genesis 1:28a NKJV).

Delight yourself also in the Lord, and He shall give you the desires of your heart (Psalm 37:4 NKJV).

The Lord is my light and my salvation; whom shall I fear? The Lord is the strength of my life; of whom shall I be afraid? (Psalm 27:1 NKJV)

God has not given us a spirit of fear, but of power and of love and of a sound mind (2 Timothy 1:7 NKJV).

Fear not, for I am with you; be not dismayed, for I am your God. I will strengthen you, yes, I will help you, I will uphold you with My righteous right hand (Isaiah 41:10 NKJV).

All you who fear God, how blessed you are! how happily you walk on His smooth straight road. You worked hard and deserve all you've got coming. Enjoy the blessing! Revel in the goodness! Your wife will bear children as a vine bears grapes, your household lush as a vineyard, the children around your table as fresh and promising as young olive shoots. Stand in awe of God's Yes. Oh, how He blesses the one who fears God! Enjoy the good life in Jerusalem every day of your life. And enjoy your grandchildren. Peace to Israel! (Psalm 128 TM)

God can do anything, you know—far more than you could ever imagine or guess or request in your wildest dreams! He does it not by pushing us around but by working within us, His Spirit deeply and gently within us (Ephesians 3:20 TM).

There has never been the slightest doubt in my mind that the God who started this great work in you would keep at it and bring it to a flourishing finish on the very day Christ Jesus appears (Philippians 1:6 TM).

I have raised you up for this very purpose, that I might display My power in you and that My name might be proclaimed in all the earth (Romans 9:17 NIV).

~ Twelve Faith-Filled Confessions of a Pregnant Covenant Woman ~

1. I shall have a perfect, healthy, normal pregnancy.

2. The Lord will lead me to the right doctor and/or midwife and will provide financially for every need.

3. I cover my placenta, uterus, and umbilical cord with the Blood of Jesus. The Blood purifies everything that goes into baby and me.

4. I will not have stretch marks, varicose veins, dry skin, puffy ankles, morning sickness, gestational diabetes, anemia, toxemia, placenta previa, spotting, cramping, hemorrhaging, depression, or any other negative symptom of pregnancy.

5. I choose to yield to the fruit of the Spirit, self-control. My emotions and appetites are healthy and God-pleasing.

6. I will not gain more than _____ pounds and will quickly return to my ideal weight after the baby is born.

7. The baby is positioned correctly and will come out head first, face down and will

rotate properly. The umbilical cord is the perfect length and will not harm the baby.

8. I will have a short, easy, painless, supernatural labor and delivery with no tearing or complications.

9. I claim Psalm 91 for my husband, our baby, and me.

10. We will have a happy, smiling, pleasant, fully matured baby that is easy to take care of.

11. We will be joyful over the gender of our baby. The Lord will give us the name He has predestined for our child.

12. We are tithing, scriptural parents who walk together in love and agreement. We have wisdom to bring up our child in the nurture and admonition of the Lord.

·– *Notes on Chapter Bridges* –·

Chapter 1 xxviii
a   "The Lady Is a Child" from the Grammy and Dove Award nominated recording *The Lady Is a Child* on Benson Records. Lyrics by Reba Rambo, music by Reba Rambo and Ron Oates. 1978 Heartwarming and Jes Fine Music.

Chapter 2 16
b   Jeremiah 29:11-14 AMP

Chapter 3 22
c   "Afraid" poem by Reba Rambo-McGuire 2001 Rambo-McGuire Publishing.

Chapter 4 30
Chapter 5 40
Chapter 6 48
Chapter 7 58
Chapter 8 80
d   "Can We Agree to Disagree?" from the recording *Suddenly* on Word Records. Lyrics and music by Reba Rambo & Dony McGuire. 1993 New Kingdom Music.

Chapter 9 96
e   "Don't Give Up" from the Grammy and Dove Award nominated recording *Confessions* on Light Records. Lyrics and music by Reba Rambo-McGuire & Dony McGuire. 1980 Lexicon, Makanume, Libris & Ooh's & Ah's.

Chapter 10 116
Chapter 11 128
f   Proverbs 18:20-21 TM

Chapter 12 140
g   "Forgive Me" from the Grammy and Dove Award winning recording *The Lord's Prayer* on Light Records. Lyrics and music by Reba Rambo-McGuire & Dony McGuire. 1980 Lexicon, Makanume, Libris and Ooh's & Ah's.

Chapter 13 150
h   "The Voice" poem by Reba Rambo-McGuire. 2001 Rambo-McGuire Publishing.

Chapter 14 156
i   "Wounded Soldier" from the Grammy and Dove Award nominated *The Bride* on Benson Records. Lyrics and music by Reba Rambo & Dony McGuire. 1983 New Kingdom Music & Benson Music.

Chapter 15 166
j   "Prodigal" poem by Reba Rambo-McGuire. 2001 Rambo-McGuire Publishing.

Chapter 16 178
k   "The Prodigal According to Reba" from the Grammy and Dove Award nominated recording *The Prodigal According to Reba* on Benson Records. Lyrics by Reba Rambo. Music by Reba Rambo and Ron Oates. 1979 Benson Publishing, Ooh's & Ah's and Jes Fine Music.

Chapter 17 202
l   "A Perfect Heart" from the Grammy and Dove Award nominated recording *Confessions* on Light Records. Lyrics and music by Reba Rambo-McGuire & Dony McGuire. 1980 Lexicon, Makanume, Libris & Ooh's & Ah's.

Chapter 18 216
m   "Because of Whose I Am" from the Grammy and Dove Award nominated recording *Confessions* on Light Records. Lyrics and music by Reba Rambo-McGuire & Dony McGuire. 1980 Lexicon, Makanume, Libris & Ooh's & Ah's.

Epilogue 232
n   "The Only Snow" from the Grammy Award nominated recording *Plain & Simple Truth* on Benson Records. Lyrics and music by Reba Rambo-McGuire & Dony McGuire. 1983 New Kingdom Music.

·~ Recommended Reading ~·

- *Power of a Praying Wife* by Stormie Omartian (Harvest House, 1997)
- *Changes That Heal* by Dr. Henry Cloud (Zondervan Publishing, 1990)
- *Boundaries* by Dr. Henry Cloud and John Townsend (Zondervan Publishing, 1992)*
- *Tired of Trying to Measure Up* by Jeff VanVonderen (Bethany House, 1989)
- *I Kissed Dating Good-bye* by Joshua Harris (Multnomah Publishers, 1997)
- *No More Sheets!* by Juanita Bynum (Pneuma Life Publishing, 1998)
- *Life Strategies* by Dr. Phillip C. McGraw (Hyperion Books, 1999)*
- *Relationship Rescue* by Dr. Phillip C. McGraw (Hyperion Books, 2000)*
- *A Woman's Guide to Breaking Bondages* by Quinn Sherrer and Ruthanne Garlock (Servant Publications, 1991)
- *Breaking Generational Curses* by Marilyn Hickey (Marilyn Hickey Ministries, 2001)
- *An Affair of the Mind* by Laurie Sharlene Hall (Focus on the Family Publishing, 1998)
- *Battlefield of the Mind* by Joyce Meyer (Harrison House, 1995)
- *The God Chasers* by Tommy Tenney (Destiny Image Publishers, 1998)*
- *God's Favorite House* by Tommy Tenney (Destiny Image Publishers, 1999)*

- *What You Say Is What You Get* by Don Gossett (Whitaker House/Anchor Books, 1976)
- *The Voice of God* by Cindy Jacobs (Regal Books, 1995)
- *Surprised by the Voice of God* by Jack Deere (Zondervan Publishing, 1996)
- *Woman, Thou Art Loosed!* by T.D. Jakes (Destiny Image Publishers, 1993)*
- *Supernatural Childbirth* by Jackie Maize (Harrison House, 1993)
- *Faith-to-Faith Devotional* by Kenneth and Gloria Copeland (Harrison House, 2000)
- *The Assignment* by Mike Murdock (Albury Publishing, 1997)
- *Developing the Leader Within* by John Maxwell (Thomas Nelson, 1993)
- *The Making of a Leader* by Frank Damazio (Trilogy Productions, 1990)
- *God@Work* by Rich Marshall (Destiny Image Publishers, 2000)
- *The Agreement* by Thomas Michael (Falcon Publishing, 2000)

* I highly recommend the companion workbook as well.

To contact the authors, please write to
PO Box 50508
Nashville, TN 37205
or visit the website at
www.rambomcguire.org

Best-Selling Author
Tommy Tenney

◢━━ HOW TO BE A GOD CHASER AND A KID CHASER
with Thetus Tenney.
One of the great challenges for the modern parent is how to make room for your personal pursuit of God in the midst of the pressing priorities of raising a family. *How to Be a God Chaser and a Kid Chaser* offers many practical answers to this challenging issue. Those answers come from a diverse background of writers including Thetus Tenney, Tommy Tenney, Ceci Sheets, Cindy Jacobs, Beth Alves, Jane Hansen, Dick Eastman, Wes and Stacey Campbell.
ISBN 0-7684-5006-3

◢━━ CHASING GOD, SERVING MAN
Chasing God, Serving Man examines the great arena of conflict that involves the world's forced segregation of the "spiritual" from the "secular." Without the mediation of Christ Jesus, these two opposites continue to repel one another, whether it is in the Church, the workplace, or the home. Tenney calls for a forging together of the passion for God and compassion for man. This will take a divine encounter somewhere between Martha's kitchen and Mary's worship.
ISBN 0-7684-5007-1

◢━━ THE GOD CHASERS (Best-selling **Destiny Image** book)
There are those so hungry, so desperate for His presence, that they become consumed with finding Him. Their longing for Him moves them to do what they would otherwise never do: Chase God. But what does it really mean to chase God? Can He be "caught"? Is there an end to the thirsting of man's soul for Him? Meet Tommy Tenney— God chaser. Join him in his search for God. Follow him as he ignores the maze of religious tradition and finds himself, not chasing God, but to his utter amazement, caught by the One he had chased.
ISBN 0-7684-2016-4
Also available in Spanish
ISBN 0-7899-0642-2
Support books available
God Chasers Daily Meditation & Personal Journal; ISBN 0-7684-2040-7
God Chasers Study Guide; ISBN 0-7684-2105-5

◢━━ GOD'S FAVORITE HOUSE
The burning desire of your heart can be fulfilled. God is looking for people just like you. He is a Lover in search of a people who will love Him in return. He is far more interested in you than He is interested in a building. He would hush all of Heaven's hosts to listen to your voice raised in heartfelt love songs to Him. This book will show you how to build a house of worship within, fulfilling your heart's desire and His!
ISBN 0-7684-2043-1

◢━━ SECRET SOURCES OF POWER
by T.F. Tenney with Tommy Tenney.
Everyone is searching for power. People are longing for some external force to empower their lives and transform their circumstances. *Secret Sources of Power* furnishes some of the keys that will unlock the door to Divine power. You might be surprised at what is on the other side of that door. It will be the opposite of the world's concepts of power and how to obtain it. You will discover that before you lay hold of God's power you must let go of your own resources. You will be challenged to go down before you can be lifted up. Death always comes before resurrection. If you are dissatisfied with your life and long for the power of God to be manifested in you then now is the time. Take the keys and open the door to *Secret Sources of Power*!
ISBN 0-7684-5000-4

Available at your local Christian bookstore.

For more information and sample chapters, visit www.destinyimage.com